PRESTON BAILEY'S
Design for Entertaining

PRESTON BAILEY'S
Design for Entertaining

INSPIRATION FOR CREATING
THE PARTY OF YOUR DREAMS

PRESTON BAILEY *with* MARIE TIMELL

Photographs by Roger Dong

and Alex Kirkbride

BULFINCH PRESS

AOL Time Warner Book Group

Boston   New York   London

To Vincent Wolf and the late Bob Patino.

Thank you for sending me on this wonderful journey.

———————

CONTENTS

INTRODUCTION

In the more than twenty years that I have been helping people to plan and design the decor of their events, I have been lucky to participate in the celebration of some of life's greatest milestones. Whether an event is a birthday or anniversary celebration, a party held by a business firm to honor clients, a fashion show, or a wedding, every one is a special occasion and cause for celebration. Because parties mark some of life's most important and intimate moments, ensuring the success of such events is a priority for everyone. People always want their event to be perfect and special, something that gives joy and pleasure to those in attendance. Sometimes, though, because it matters so much and because there is so much to do, people don't know where to begin or what to do when they first start to think about hosting an event.

Staging an event can be quite an art. In essence, you don't plan a party as much as you design it. Planning an event is a production: the venue and setting are the stage, the hostess, the director. If all of this leaves you at a loss at the outset — that's where I come in. I help my clients articulate a vision or mood for an event and then make it a reality. Together we go through the process of envisioning and creating an entire environment for their guests from scratch, one that will be both exciting and memorable — in essence, an experience. My goal in planning any event is to elicit an emotional, even passionate, response from the guests while inventing an environment that is meaningful and personal for my client.

In generating an event's overall concept, much of my role is to encourage my clients to broaden their vision and engage in the creative process while at the same time easing any fears they may have. Any act of creation can be wonderful but may feel a bit chaotic at first. And since all events are celebrations of one kind or another, why be fearful or worried that it won't be a success? I approach designing an event as an adventure, and I encourage my clients to have fun with it, as I do.

Most of what I have learned about creativity has come from Mother Nature — my work with flowers. I began my career as a floral designer. As a child growing up in Panama, I was surrounded by beautiful tropical flowers. Wild orchids lined the streets of the neighborhood where I lived. As a young adult, I moved to New York, became a model, and was involved in fashion. Later, quite by accident, I tried my hand at arranging flowers and became quite passionate about it. I started haunting the flower district to learn as much as I could about the different varieties of flowers and traveling around the city to various public venues such as the Metropolitan Museum of Art to observe their floral arrangements. As part of my education, I studied books on botany and horticulture, and also books on art history, architecture, and design in general.

Experience taught me to trust my instincts, and as I did, my creativity expanded in many new directions. My thinking moved beyond flowers as I developed a broader perspective about my clients' needs. I started to think of arrangements less in terms of decoration and more in terms of decor. I came to understand that flowers are just a part of the overall decor in a space and that they could be used to enhance and uplift a decor or design concept and even to inspire a new design idea altogether.

This "total decor concept" was very successful for me, and before long I was being asked to assist my clients with their special events. I started my entertainment and set design business in 1986, and since then I have worked with countless individuals to help them conceptualize and design their important celebrations and parties. Another side of my work includes set design for photo shoots and fashion shows. My business clients have been as diverse as *Glamour* magazine, Victoria's Secret, and Wall Street investment firms. I consider myself lucky to have worked with many clients who are known for their exquisite personal style, including a number of well-known celebrities. I count among my individual clients Oprah Winfrey, Michael Douglas and Catherine Zeta-Jones, football great Emmitt Smith III, Disney executive Robert Iger and his wife, television anchorwoman Willow Bay, fashion designer John Galliano, and Mrs. Bill Cosby, among others. I designed the wedding setting for NBC *Today* show host Matt Lauer and his wife, Annette Roque, and for Joan Rivers's daughter, Melissa. When Oprah launched her magazine, *O,* she asked me to plan the party.

In the pages that follow, I describe my thinking and process when I conceptualize and design an event. My goals are twofold: first, to give you a framework for your thoughts about your event and, second, and more important, to encourage you to allow your creativity to blossom. Whether you are working with professionals or managing all the details yourself, I want to help you give the most spectacular, memorable, and fun event possible. I lead you through all the phases of designing the perfect party. In the first chapter I discuss how to generate ideas to develop a concept for an event and I encourage you to expand your thinking and creativity. The most successful events are always those that reflect who you are and your own personal style. In chapter 2 I talk about how to create an overall mood for your event by working with color and texture. Light can be key in effecting mood, and in chapter 3 I discuss different ways to think about lighting and give you some pointers on this important but easily overlooked aspect of event design.

The decision about the location or venue for your event is crucial because this becomes the canvas on which you will then apply your ideas and vision. Chapter 4 demonstrates how I think about a room and shows you how dramatically a space can be transformed. Chapters 5 and 6 discuss the details of event decor, what to do in different problem situations, and how to think about flowers. Lastly, in chapter 7 I walk you through five unique events that truly made a statement and that I was privileged to design. Each is a wonderful lesson in how to make a party extraordinary.

While you may be inspired by the many ideas presented in the text and photos here, I hope this book also helps to transform your thinking. Rather than your being uncertain or nervous about your upcoming event, perhaps reading this book will give you confidence about your own sense of style and encouragement to take some risks. Trust your creative instincts, and designing your event is sure to be an inspired and therefore enjoyable process. Since I love what I do, it is my hope that I can share that with you.

— PRESTON BAILEY

PRESTON BAILEY'S
Design for Entertaining

Chapter 1

ENVISIONING THE EVENT

SOURCES OF INSPIRATION

"What is the overall impression you'd like to convey to your guests?" I ask when working with my clients. "What statement would you like to make?" Most clients know the answer but have difficulty expressing it. Or they are able to answer with a word or two that encapsulate what they have in mind but haven't a clue how to make their idea a reality. What I do in my work as a designer of event decor is to help my clients conceptualize and articulate a vision or style and then communicate this to their guests. In this chapter I show you how I work with my clients to achieve that deeply personal touch so that you will be inspired to do the same for your own events, large or small.

What makes an event a success?

In the course of my career I have helped my clients design some of their most special occasions. For me an event is a success when, long afterward, people experience a feeling of joy when they remember it. Moreover, what comes back to mind for them isn't so much specific details as an overall sense of the event's theme, ambience, and mood. In short, they recall that they have had a unique and uplifting experience, one punctuated by certain emotional highlights. And this is really at the heart of what every host or hostess hopes to achieve. Everyone wants a special event to be a success. And the most successful events are always the ones that leave a long-lasting impression.

Before planning an event—whether a wedding, dinner, anniversary, birthday celebration, or business affair—consider what overall effect you are hoping to achieve. More than the details, the location, or the food, it is the overall feeling that will be remembered. The ambience you create is vital because, whether consciously or not, your guests will absorb it during the course of your event. An event's decor is an environment, womblike, that for some short period of time envelopes and nurtures your guests, feeds them and entertains them. And in so doing you are influencing how they will feel and what they will remember in the years to come. What is the overall impression you'd like to convey?

Almost all events are occasions for celebration, and as such they are always, no matter how large, intimate occasions. This is because you are sharing something special to you with people that you care about. So it is natural for you to wish to ensure the success of your event and that your guests have a wonderful experience. The intimate relationship that exists between the host or hosts of an event and their guests is one I work with and try to honor and respect, and you should too. By inviting your guests to partake in your occasion, you are giving of yourself. Generosity of spirit should be your main goal. All else follows from there. Give as much of yourself as possible to ensure a truly memorable event. Show who you are, and your guests are certain to be touched. Remember, whether your party is a wedding or a corporate luncheon for clients, you are gathering together people that are important to you. There is no better way to show that you care than to give generously of yourself. Better yet, communicate a sense of joy and you will make your event an experience your guests will remember for a lifetime.

When you design an event or its theme, you are surrounding your guests with a part of who you are—in fact, with your own deeply held sense of style. Keep this in mind as encouragement to make every effort

Re-creating the Decor of a Home

Here is an example of an event that is a deeply personal statement. My clients, a couple, were giving a joint birthday celebration for friends and family. To accommodate their many guests they raised a tent on their property. But their aim was to make their guests feel as though they had been invited into their home for this intimate occasion. Owing to the hostess's distinctive sense of style and the couple's generosity of spirit, we literally re-created the decor of their home for the party. Though it may be hard to imagine, this festive table duplicates the colors, linens, and architectural details within their home so perfectly, one can hardly believe this table setting is in a tent. Even the image of the vase with the floral arrangement on the wall is a photograph of one in their home!

to express yourself. There is an added benefit to this as well. It can represent the difference between a fine party and one that is truly unique. What could be more personal than your own combination of likes and dislikes? If you start from the center of who you are and stay true to your self, you are unlikely to duplicate anything that anyone has ever done before. Your guests are certain to be charmed and excited by what you create because it is unlikely to be in any way ordinary.

Another measure of the success of any party, event, or celebration is in how it leaves your guests feeling. You want those in attendance to experience a myriad of uplifting emotions during the course of the event, ranging from excitement to elation. In addition, your guests may experience joy, surprise; feel deeply touched or amused; as well as be entertained. How you conceive of your event, how you manage the ambience you create for your guests, will have an impact on their feelings. When a party is designed and planned properly, it will be the range of emotional reactions that makes your party memorable.

Designing a theme — what matters to you?

One of the most important things I do for my clients is to help them express what they are aiming for, to articulate their own vision. When I sit down to work with a client, first we discuss the type of event that is being planned, then we think about style, and ultimately a concept or theme develops, including color and mood. The key is to be as original as you can and to design something as different as possible so long as that reflects who you are and what you are comfortable with. My staff and I are always trying to think of ways to translate what the client wants and then to create it from scratch so that it will be wholly original.

Usually I encourage my clients to come up with one or two words, keywords, that represent the effect they are interested in achieving. While I have begun the design process with many different keywords, from romantic to masculine to lighthearted, by far the most common

Inspiration from India at a Luncheon for Joan Rivers

Excited by her experiences during a recent trip to India, Joan Rivers gave a luncheon for thirty of her closest friends to share her journey. Naturally, Indian cuisine was served, and the decor of the event reflected the richness, colors, textures, tastes, and architecture of that country. Joan encouraged me to pull out all the stops to make the event as abundant and diverse as the country itself. We began by creating large-scale floral sculptures for the table and buffet, one in the shape of an elephant, a reminder of the Indian god of fortune, Ganesh; several in the shape of a peacock; and one reflecting the dome shapes found in Indian architecture and calling to mind the Taj Mahal. We covered the elephant with masses of green daisies and a saddle made of roses. In playful attention to detail, beads were wound around the elephant's neck and on the other sculptures as well.

An eclectic mix of different-colored votives, all with silver filigree, cast a warm glow over the proceedings. Bedecked with several fuchsia saris as linen, the table was set with gold-leafed terra-cotta chargers and fine silver. And a profusion of hot-colored dahlias and water lilies, just like those found in depictions of Indian deities, were scattered over the table in a variety of containers to mimic India's rich diversity. As a final touch, for good luck, Joan gave a miniature Indian elephant to each of her guests.

word I hear is elegant. You'd be surprised how many different notions people have of what that is. Moreover, elegance can be translated in many ways. For example, it can be understated or very elaborate, simple or traditional. It is up to me to enable my clients to pinpoint what elegance means to them and to execute that.

One gentleman came to me with a very specific vision for his daughter's wedding. For him, elegance was about simplicity and the use of white. For my client, white French tulips represent an ideal of elegance, with their long willow-colored stems and the perfection and simplicity of their oversized petals. Because they had a meaning for him, we designed a room around these flowers, mirroring their shape, color, and elegance wherever we could. To match the petals of the flowers and to frame them, we covered the room in white: drapes, table linens, tableware, and seat covers. And on every table, in sparklingly clear, crystal vases, we placed magnificent groupings of the beloved French tulips that had been specially flown in for the wedding.

In many ways what I do is a cross between interior design and set decoration. Just as an interior designer translates someone's personal style onto the interior of a home, I transmit their style to the decor of their party. My relationship with a client is just as intimate as that between you and your interior decorator, though of course that is a much longer relationship. The set design analogy comes into play in the sense that event decor is also a one-time situation, one designed to leave a specific, abiding impression on an audience.

Style is versatile; it can be anything for anyone. For some it is colorful and dynamic, while for others it is pared-down-to-the-essentials simplicity. Any special occasion is an opportunity for you reflect on or play with your own personal style. Style is a buzzword today, but its importance cannot be overestimated. Style is a personal statement, since it represents what is of interest or matters to you. It is also an act of creation, because you as the creator are assembling those elements into a coherent and, it is hoped, harmonious whole. To me style is a kind of

Perfect Understated Simplicity

For this wedding reception our mandate was to design an environment of "elegant simplicity." This was a bit of a challenge, since the event was to be held in the ballroom of the Plaza Hotel in New York, which is noted for its classic and ornate gilt detailing. So we opted to work with the decor as opposed to against it. Thus, the primary color theme of the event was pure white with gold and silver. The tables were white — raw silk overlays on fine cotton, white napkins, and white tableware. Typically, a monochromatic color scheme such as this makes for pure elegance. We rented silver ballroom chairs for the event to match the tables and gave them sturdy white seat covers. We even covered the strongly colored burgundy drapes in the room with white fabric.

Clear crystal trumpet vases were the perfect understated containers for the white French tulips specially flown in for the wedding. That was it. White. Gold. Silver. And masses of French tulips placed high in the already tall vases, bowing gracefully over the tables. The upward movement of the tulips and the thin forms of their stems were mirrored by the twenty-four-inch taper candles surrounding each arrangement. The effect: simple and elegant but also worthy of King Louis XIV's court.

A Children's Party with a Technology Theme

We called this party "Jenny.com" in honor of the young lady for whom the party was given. Her parents encouraged us to make technology the theme of the event, since their daughter Jenny loves computers and the Internet. We put rented computer monitors on all the tables for the children, providing some entertainment for short attention spans while making clear the concept. Each computer showed a montage of photos of Jenny's life. We created a video collage mixing pop culture, Japanese anime, and personal photography all fused together with a techno interface. The computer graphics captivated the guests while truly delighting the guest of honor. Gifts in the form of an individual candy assortment and a futuristic pen set in a wire holder that would make George Jetson proud graced each place setting. Labeled Jenny.com, they continued the technology theme of the party. And a careful observer will notice that the colors used throughout the event pay homage to the vibrant range of colors packaged with the latest iMac hardware.

The tables for the adults did not have computers. A party for both parents and children requires a balanced design that suits kids but also keeps the adults in mind by not making the whole thing look too childish. This was achieved through the judicious use of the floral decor. Vibrant pink, red, and purple blooms were colorful and upbeat enough to provide the bold colors typical of children's events. However, the arrangements on the children's tables were pint-size, while those for the parents were large floral bouquets sitting in glass pedestals, at once more sophisticated and overstated to suit adult tastes.

A Different Thanksgiving Decor

Here is a Thanksgiving dinner with another point of view. Thanksgiving is about plenty, but the host of this event wanted a simple, restrained elegance that reflected the warm colors of the season with a unique twist. Simplicity was the main idea, but repetition, contrast, and texture provided an intriguing yet understated effect. Burned-orange roses arranged to appear to be one large rose were placed in golden-hued pedestaled glass containers — one for each place setting — and served as uncomplicated, yet lovely, floral arrangements. Masses of frosted square votives pushed together to form larger squares in repeating blocks across the table took the place of traditional centerpieces while casting the faces of guests in a shimmering light.

As a personal statement, we used some wonderful faux leopard as seat covers. It's also masculine — perfect in this case, since the host was a man. Adding texture and contrast, the print worked well with the orange raw silk tablecloth. Simple linen napkins folded in a square continued the idea of repeating squares in contrast to the repeating circular bowls of flowers. Two specially dried magnolia leaves placed on each napkin simulated hands held open in offering and were a subtle reminder of fall.

A Vineyard-Inspired Wine Tasting

The wine aficionados who hosted this lavish dinner party and wine tasting asked me to create a setting that would give the impression of being in a vineyard but that also bespoke the elegance befitting a formal sit-down dinner. Because it took place in the fall, we incorporated an autumnal theme as well. With a sommelier in attendance, the hosts served some of the best wines from around the world. In fact, discreet closed-circuit screens on each table provided intimate access to the sommelier's discussion of each wine.

To transform the venue, arborlike structures were built to frame the tables. Grapevines and amaranthus were draped from them, gently reaching down toward the tables laden with black grapes and rich jewel-toned flowers. Long rectangular tables accommodating up to twenty-five people each were used, since they afforded greater accessibility for waiters as wine was poured and dinner served. For the same reason, as well as to allow room for the many wineglasses, the tables were kept free of candles. Dramatic branch sculptures laden with grapes, roses, and wisteria, cattleya orchids, hydrangeas, and calla lilies, composed the centerpieces. Tablecloths of rich cognac-colored velvet embossed with a leaf pattern set off gold chargers, napkins, and tableware. Place cards in the shape of a leaf were furnished by a graphic designer. And as a finishing touch, we sprinkled the tables with festive paper leaves in a myriad of fall colors. The overall richness of the event was reminiscent of the feasting at rustic banquets to celebrate the successful completion of the harvest in days gone by.

joyful flow between the inner person and presentation of the outer person. Successfully extending this flow even further onto your event will leave your guests feeling closer to you, happy, and satisfied.

Much of what I do involves exploration and translation. I encourage my clients to set aside their fears and explore what style means to them as freely as possible. Often this entails helping them understand what makes them comfortable and then working to translate it into something with style. When I interview clients I ask them about their likes and dislikes. I look for clues as to the style in their home. Is the decor elaborate or understated? I ask my clients about their favorite color schemes. Certain people love pastels and creams, while others are totally passionate about vibrant color. These preferences are important because clients must feel absolutely comfortable with the decor created for their event. If you create an environment that makes you feel at home, then your guests will feel at home as well.

Even for a business event, comfort can come into play. A company's management may not be comfortable creating an over-the-top or lavish affair for clients or owners for fear of appearing to be spendthrifts. On the other hand, a company may not wish to seem overly budget conscious and appear as though they don't value their guests. Balance, as always, is the best guide, but finding your comfort level is crucial.

Developing a unique vision

As you start to think about what idea, keyword, or theme you'd like to have inform your event, keep in mind that it should matter to you. Put all limitations aside for the time being. And do not consider what anyone else will think. Free your spirit. Permit yourself to become enchanted by the possibilities. Indulge your quirks, and more than anything: break the rules! If you plan to nurture, value, and honor your guests, then offer these qualities to yourself as you begin the planning process. Lis-

A Winter Wonderland in New York City

Every Christmas a New York City executive pitches a tent in the backyard of her brownstone in which to hold a number of different events that she hosts at that time of year. Her goal each year is to give her guests a memorable event that is inspired by the season. This year's theme was the silvery frosted feeling of a winter's evening.

Our main effect was to digitally print scenes of a winter forest in silver ink onto the tent's walls. Not only did this create a distinct mood but it transformed the tent into a room, making it, in effect, an addition to the house. Shimmering silver organza overlays were thrown over raw silk underlays on the tables. Silver berries graced crisp white napkins neatly folded over elegant silver-edged chargers. Pinecones were used throughout the space, hanging from the ceiling and filling the large crystal vases used for the seasonal red, green, and white floral arrangements. We hung lit frosted pillar candles in old-fashioned glass lanterns from the tent's ceiling and placed frosted votives on the tables. Guests, surrounded by a woodland powdered with snow and silhouetted against the night sky, were enveloped in a quite specific mood — one that evoked the warmth and security of being indoors while the cold winter night outside lurks on the edge of awareness.

Bringing Nature Indoors

The gallery housing the famed Temple of Dendur at New York's Metropolitan Museum of Art was the site for this corporate dinner one evening in May. The Metropolitan sits nestled at the very edge of New York's Central Park. The hall housing the ancient Egyptian temple contains a wall of windows, as high as the room itself, that overlook the park and its many trees joyously abloom in the late spring. It was this that provided the inspiration for the decor for the event. Nature was too beautiful to be ignored. We were compelled to bring it indoors. An extravagant idea, perhaps, but it's important to find the fine line between beauty and extravagance.

Additional and important considerations in our decor concept were the temple and the gallery itself. The temple, given intact to the United States by the Egyptian government, is itself a symbol of the natural world. More important, it was dedicated to Isis, Egyptian goddess of fertility. How appropriate then to celebrate the profusion of spring that evening! The room consists of clean lines and stone, all in homage to the ancient architecture of the temple. Trying to create a decor in that room that was in any way typical of large events would have been false to the space.

Since it was our aim to bring the trees indoors, we had to create them. Monumental gold metal frames set on every table became tree trunks. Greenery, white viburnum, or snowballs, and hydrangeas simulated the blooming branches of the fruit trees in the park. The largesse of the "trees" also succeeded in filling out the space of the hall, without which the room might have lacked a sense of intimacy or warmth. Overall the effect was perfect to encourage the easy interaction of the senior management and stockholders of the company hosting this event.

ten to that little voice whispering to you. Trust your intuition. Do what you like. It's *your* party.

Sometimes the time of year comes into play when developing the design concept for an event. The seasons often influence the overall look of an affair. And certainly this is the easiest idea around which to base a theme. A Thanksgiving event will emphasize the abundance of the season; it might reflect the generosity of the harvest and be colored with the hues of autumn leaves. A spring wedding, on the other hand, might be designed around the bright promise of springtime, with pastels in pinks and greens and an overall light and airy look. Winter can inspire a more subdued environment for a gathering, one that speaks with rich crimsons set off by stark whites.

What's important is that the theme reflects your feelings, likes, and dislikes. Use the seasons as a starting place if a particular season speaks to you. If you love autumn and its rich golden colors, by all means use this as a basis for your event. But don't ever feel bound by the time of year. Use it only if it means something to you.

One of my clients is a woman whose self-assurance in terms of her own tastes and style is simply inspiring. She's a lesson to us all because she allows herself the luxury of indulging what she likes. Because she loves pink and blue, her exquisite home is decorated entirely in these two colors in an amazing array of textures, fabrics, and mediums. But they are not just any pink and blue. They are such specific hues that I wouldn't even attempt to describe them in words. She has surrounded herself and her family with what she loves. So, why stop there? When she and her husband decided to create a joint birthday celebration, she decided the concept for her party should be an extension of this same theme. Pink and blue. So she had me re-create the design and theme of her home. The effect was fabulous and breathtaking. And her guests were left feeling as though they had truly been invited into her life and its celebration.

Adding Texture and Scent

To tickle the senses with springtime, we placed white gardenias around the room so guests would be greeted by their tantalizing scent upon entering. Because we were using two simple colors for this event, it was important to contribute as much texture as possible. The floral configurations were extraordinarily textured and organic, and we wanted the fabrics used for the event to be as well. The table linens carried a design that was vaguely Egyptian in feeling without being too obvious. The sheer chair covers were interwoven with a vinelike pattern and graced with ribbons for movement. The result was a classic evening of decorum and freshness, one befitting the pharaohs as they might have dined in their gardens or made offerings to Isis under the light of a full moon in the springtime.

An African-Theme Benefit Party for Third World Women

This party was a benefit held by the Foundation for International Community Assistance (FINCA), a provider of small loans and other financial services to low-income families in developing nations all over the world. Among the many prominent women who were involved were then First Lady Hillary Clinton and Queen Rania al-Abdullah of Jordan.

Since the ultimate recipients of the evening's fund-raising would be grassroots businesses and families, we wanted to convey an earthy and organic theme for the party — as well as the international focus. For that we were inspired by African themes. Table coverings of different-hued cloth seemingly inspired by African designs were used as overlays to the elegance of black tablecloths. Adorning the tables were organic branch-and-vine sculptures decorated only with orchids — cymbidium and cattleya — among nature's most luscious flowers. Each place setting was also adorned with a simple apricot-colored orchid sitting demurely on a crisp white napkin. Adding to the organic feel of the evening was the giant tree we constructed in the center of the room. Meanwhile, jasmine scented the room, leaving its indelible fragrance in the memory of guests long after they'd returned home.

I always ask my clients to think about color, the importance of which should never be underestimated. Most people have specific feelings about color; there are often colors that they don't like, that they, in fact, have an aversion to, perhaps due to childhood memories. Or they might just be tired of a particular color. Alternatively, people also, naturally, have favorite colors and can be quite adamant about using them. Then there are those who are indifferent to color and care more about style. But there have been occasions when a color or colors became the main theme of an event. Just that. Red. Blue. White. But as can be expected, weaving this theme through the whole affair can be quite whimsical and fun.

To develop the concept for an event, I also recommend that you study different books and magazines on art, interior design, fashion, and architecture. Think about your favorite movies and which historical periods attract you. Consider which clothing designers you like or feel reflect your style. You might even take an objective look at the clothes that make you feel most comfortable. Look at their lines. Are they sleek or subdued? Brightly colored with lots of detailing? At the beginning focus on simply gathering together ideas, and be sure not to limit yourself. The more fearless you are, the more original you will be. Realize that anything is possible. Just try to develop a feel for what resonates with you. Pursue any ideas that give you a sense of energy and passion without worrying about the execution. Leave the "hows" behind for a while and let inspiration be your guide. If you want something a little different, it's better to challenge yourself a bit and worry about the details later. If some aspect of what you envision isn't available to you, there are always creative alternatives. If you are worried about your budget, you'd be surprised at how much can be created for you for not much more. Soon you'll realize that everything falls into place and a vision of what you want will present itself to you.

$\mathscr{S}$HAPING YOUR VISION
TO CREATE A MOOD

Once the concept for an event is established, I start to think about ways to translate it into a reality. A large part of this process is communicating the desired mood of an event. The range of mood is as broad as the range of emotions: will the mood of your event be subdued and refined or light-hearted and bursting with energy? I help my clients create the mood or overall emotional tone for their occasions. We set the stage for the event, much like the director of a film or a play that elicits an emotional response from an audience.

A mood can be crafted, shaped and molded. When shaping a mood, you are acting a lot like a sculptor, only you are working with color, texture, and light. Seemingly indefinable, mood is familiar to everyone. "That puts me in a good mood," someone says. Mood is a kind of energy, and like energy, it is difficult to define, yet everyone seems to know what it is. Interestingly, *mood* is one of those words that can be used to describe both the emotional state of an individual and the exterior atmosphere. This duality and the connection between the two is what is crucial. What makes mood so important is its subtlety. Mood's effect on an event is both subtle and enormous and can best be likened to the process of osmosis. Done correctly, the mood created for an event will impress itself on the guests so that it becomes their mood as well.

Color's influence on mood

One of the most important ways to affect a mood is through color. Though everyone has favorite or least favorite colors, certain colors are associated with specific moods, and it is best to keep this in mind while planning. As you start to think about the decor of your party, it is as though you were contemplating a blank canvas on which you will apply broad and important swashes of color.

When choosing color, you may wish to simply pick the colors that are your favorites. You already know which colors appeal to you, but keep in mind that how you express color is also important. For example, red can be expressed both as elegant and subdued and as scintillating and passionate. Consider the purpose of your event when selecting your palette. As most of us know, different colors convey different emotions. Though a certain color may be a favorite of yours, it may not be appropriate to the event in question.

One of the most popular color palettes I'm asked to work with is white or white in combination with pastels. In my experience white is the most comfortable color for the majority of people. The purity and simplicity associated with white often denote dignity and elegance. Because white is so pristine, I've noticed it does affect tone in a profound way. White's usual association with a certain decorum makes it often requested for elegant dinners and wedding ceremonies. But more than anything else, it is its versatility that is most noteworthy; white can be both traditional and contemporary. Another popular palette is a combination of tints in lighter colors — creams, pale pinks, pale lavenders. These more muted colors are often associated with romance.

Then there are the wonderful hot colors. Some people love reds and oranges; these colors excite them. Hot colors add energy, drive, and verve to an event. In contrast, the cool colors — blues, greens, and lavenders — impart a smoothness or sleekness to an environment and

A Red Wedding Reception

Annette Roque was very specific about the color scheme she wanted for her wedding reception with NBC *Today* show cohost Matt Lauer. She envisioned a decor of reds and burgundies with simple lines. Exotic for a wedding, and deeply romantic, the use of only red heightened its intensity and created a mood that was both dramatic and sensual.

Though dinner was held in a tent, Annette asked me to make the interior look like a room. We brought in yards and yards of gorgeous deep crimson raw silk to swathe and drape the inside with both color and texture. The silk was also used as the table overlays, making the room that much more exciting visually. Bowing to Annette's desire for clean lines, we kept the tables as simple as possible (page 40). The centerpieces, though highly textural, were traditional and low, set in silver-footed containers and made up entirely of deep red blooms, with the occasional purple flower added. Burgundy cattleya orchids graced the floral arrangements as well as the place settings. Groupings of squat pillar candles in reds and purples were neat and to the point while also being different.

The most dramatic touch of the decor was the dozens of Asian paper lanterns we hung from the ceiling, each with a single electric bulb within, giving the room an exaggerated red glow. The lanterns bounced gently, creating the allure of movement and drawing the eye upward. The mood of this special evening, unmistakably one of love and passion, was not soon forgotten by guests.

create an ambience that is quite calming, perhaps even soothing. Marvelous jewel tones — ruby, emerald, sapphire — can betoken a traditional richness and beneficence.

Of course there are also the classic associations. Pink is considered feminine and romantic, while blue may be more masculine. It may be hard to get away from this. But today it's okay to break all the rules, and I encourage my clients to do so. For example, certain colors are associated with certain seasons. But it isn't a requirement to use light pastel colors in spring and warm reds and oranges in the fall. You can really twist things around and do what you want. However, if you love the colors of autumn and want to base your fall event around them, do so.

It can be interesting to heighten the intensity of emotion or mood by using a palette of analogous colors. In other words, keeping the color scheme of your event monochromatic. For example, combining red, orange, and magenta or blue, blue-violet, and purple would magnify the mood connected to the main color of red or blue.

When bringing different colors together, be sure that you select those that will act in harmony with each other. Inharmonious color combinations can cause tension and a disjointed feeling at an event. Inharmonious colors are not necessarily opposites on the color wheel, such as red and green or yellow and violet. Opposites can, in fact, heighten the intensity of each other. Dissonant or inharmonious colors are colors that aren't next to or opposite each other on the color wheel, such as orange-red and purple. Dissonance can also be created by combining colors of different tones.

The decor of a party can involve a number of different primary color schemes. For example, if the event is a wedding, the ceremony may be decorated in classic white because white denotes a certain solemnity or spirituality. But the decor of the cocktail hour and the reception could each use entirely different, perhaps more festive or energetic, colors.

Color will influence most of the details of an event. The flowers you select for your decor will, of course, be chosen largely for their color.

A Bacchus-Inspired Stage Set for John Galliano

John Galliano, designer for Christian Dior, has won international acclaim for his theatrical, avant-garde designs and craftsmanship. He is also known for the unusual settings he chooses for the display of his latest collections. Meticulous in his attention to detail, for this fashion show he chose to create a set piece of bacchanalian proportions. Exhibiting a winter line, he envisioned something truly elaborate. Rather than have models walk out to parade before the audience, he wanted them sitting in various positions around a huge table, as though they were in the midst of a joyously abundant dinner party. This is a painterly effect — a mise-en-scène — within which he even created a variety of vignettes. The audience entered the room where all this was already taking place and stood or sat around the periphery of the room, observing the scene and the stories within it.

The overall mood of Galliano's show was one of rich abundance and organic opulence, all enhanced by a veritable cornucopia of texture and color. The luxuriousness of this room at New York's Metropolitan Club only contributed to the overall effect, one fit for Bacchus himself, god of wine, fertility, and ecstatic frenzy.

Your linens, draping, tableware, and other decorative details will also be selected to fit into your overall color scheme. This doesn't mean that you have to select one color and everything must be that color — though this is an interesting effect. Instead, select a palette of colors and work from there. Add and subtract as you go along. Color is fascinating; enjoy it!

Using texture to invoke sensuality

Any party is most successful when it is a feast for the senses. Texture is the key ingredient for tickling the senses and heightening mood. By texture, I mean anything that elicits some sensory response. Touch, vision, and smell will all be affected in some way when texture is used to good effect in shaping the overall mood of an event. Flowers, fabrics, and scent all create texture. Fluffy billows of overripe peonies generate a sense memory of softness and voluptuousness. The sheen of satin tablecloths or overlays reminds guests of the silky smoothness of the fabric's feel on the skin. The scent of jasmine adds an air of mystery and transports people to exotic locales.

The use of texture is a sophisticated way to be creative and inventive in communicating your key ideas and mood. For example, one of the best ways to communicate generosity of spirit is through the overuse of texture. Brocades or rich patterns, fabrics of satin, silk, organza, or velvet, beading, tassels, or other details, and flowers that are highly textural communicate voluptuousness and abundance. On the other hand, if you want a clean or contemporary look, you would keep the lines in your decor minimal and your textures smooth.

By its nature, texture is sensual; thus it is also intimate. Since you want to give your best to your guests, you are likely to choose your favorite linens, tableware, stemware, and other silver, containers and other decor elements. These will be the items that feel good to you, per-

A Wedding Ceremony Fit for the Czars

Inspired by the Hermitage and Czarist Russia in winter, the wedding ceremony prepared by Joan Rivers for her only daughter, Melissa, had all of New York talking for months. The mood Joan wanted for the ceremony portion of the wedding was the nearly sacred, awe-inspiring feeling of a clear, star-filled night in the depths of winter. We created a winter wonderland for the event. Against a backdrop of cobalt blue lighting concocted by a lighting designer, we created rows of twenty-foot-high white birch trees for the ceremony aisle and lit them from below. The room's existing chandeliers worked beautifully with the canopy created by the trees. A "snowfall" consisted of affixing thousands of dainty fresh white flowers on all the tree branches and blanketing the room in a carpet of pure white. Meanwhile, the chairs and their white padded upholstery were the perfect complement to the whole event. It is interesting to note that though the room was really three levels, we made it one level for the event by building platforms across the levels. The effect was solemn, as befitted a spiritual occasion, and magically romantic.

haps even have a sense memory for you. The rule is: Use it if it feels good to you.

Fabrics come in so many luscious textures that choosing the right ones for your event can be a joy. Shimmering organza to silky-smooth satin can be used for tablecloths or overlays. Fabrics can be beaded, embroidered, or tasseled. Ribbons abound. Tablecloths that drape and puddle around tables provide one textural effect. Fabric is also important in draping and covering unsightly spaces and for swagging and poufing as a decorative element.

Because they are organic, it is the nature of flowers to arouse all the senses. This is why their use is so widespread. Flowers give you an incredible amount of texture and feeling. Though individually some blooms are more obviously textural than others, don't underestimate what happens when flowers are gathered in bunches. Texture can be created with blooms of even the simplest lines simply by bringing them together. An orchid alone is clean and simple, but when orchids are massed, they become highly textural. Florals with many ruffled petals contribute significant texture. And of course, flowers contribute fragrance to an event.

Learning to mix color and texture can be quite an art. Texture is particularly vital when you have chosen a monochromatic theme for your event; otherwise you risk a certain flatness to the overall effect. You can enliven any color scheme through the use of textural touches. If, for example, your event is entirely white or ivory, find a deeply embossed cream table linen. Use fabrics of white satin or organza for their sheen or reflection. Choose flowers in the same color family but with distinct and diverse shapes. Finding ways to create texture within a single color palette can be something of an adventure.

Among the easiest ways to generate texture is through the use of repetition or contrast. An object may be uncomplicated in form, but when repeated it becomes a type of texture. Placing the same bloom in the same vase and affixing it to a wall over and over again creates tex-

A Fund-Raiser for Meals on Wheels

Another more-serious affair was this fund-raiser for Meals on Wheels held in the basement of a prominent church. We erected a scrim to separate the entranceway from the dining area. As they arrived, guests could see the glow of dozens of raised pillar candles floating beckoningly in the other room through the organza scrim. The resulting mood was one of seriousness of intent but also evoked a certain spirituality or sense of higher purpose. The support columns were wrapped in garlands of green smilax and branches, then spotlighted for dramatic effect, which, like the candles, drew the eye and mind upward, one hopes, to loftier ideas. The tables were draped in organza over burlap underlays — a truly inspired bit of decor! Peonies, roses, and lilacs in a rustic terra-cotta container, along with five silver candleholders, completed the tables. With nothing more than a bit of organza and some candles, we conveyed a truly atmospheric and specific mood for this evening.

ture because you are interrupting the blank surface of the wall. Working with repetition is one of the simplest and least expensive ways to enliven an event and to avoid dullness. Contrast is another important way to enhance texture. Place organza over burlap and see what happens. Combine crisp linen with ruffles. Contrast needn't feel forced. Making something interesting should never take the place of an overall sense of harmony.

Texture can also involve sound, motion, and fragrance. Sound, for example, can be added with the tinkling of wind chimes or the soft gurgling of water from a fountain. Both of these, of course, contribute movement as well. Another example of movement would be paper lanterns gently swaying at the roof of a tent. Scent is a powerful stimulus, one that can arouse and titillate the senses. Its discriminating use can add much to the mood of a party. Scented candles and even incense may be used if you wish to tickle the olfactory senses of your guests. Of course, the flowers you use may contribute fragrance. Take care to understand the scents of the flowers you select for your event. Some flowers are powerfully pungent: lilies, jasmine, gardenias, and tuberoses, for example. Use them but sparingly, since you don't want to overwhelm the room.

The amount of texture you create will depend on your vision for your event. If you want to convey opulence, you will surround your guests with texture. If you want a contemporary, avant-garde feel, you will choose simple lines and less texture. You might want to use highly textured fabrics with highly textured flowers — that's one effect. This, of course, won't be as understated or chaste as a plain fabric and the repetition of a few simple blooms. It really depends on how risky a statement you want to make. Clearly, this is one place you can take risks. I think everyone should. Don't go with safety and the rules. The interesting thing is to try something and find a way to make it work. That's the challenge: making it work.

A Corporate Luncheon at the Pierpont Morgan Library

Here is an example of an event designed to have a serious mood, one for business and geared toward the masculine. It was given at the Pierpont Morgan Library, where the room's floor and walls are marble, which creates a very clean, no-nonsense effect. Keeping the event decor in line with the venue and the tone of the luncheon, we chose simple black chairs, crisp white linens for the tables, and simple silver table overlays. Even the tableware and silver were quite straightforward. We used very nearly stark centerpieces for the tables — more branch sculptures than floral arrangements, graced by just a few cattleya orchids. Pared-down elegance is perfect for a business event.

Chapter 3

Lighting and Its Effect on Mood

The important role of lighting in effecting the mood of a party is often ignored. The illumination level can enliven or subdue any event and is vital to controlling mood. Lighting is also important in the way that it works with color and actually uses color as another ingredient in decor. Lighting enables you to draw the attention of guests to where you want it and away from where you don't. All your carefully chosen decoration will go unnoticed without the proper illumination.

No matter how carefully thought out all the details of an event may be, it is lighting that can make or break a party. It can be large scale, done by a professional, and very costly. Or it can be done in a very basic way and on a budget, for instance, by using the ambient lighting of a space in conjunction with candles. The main requirement is that attention be paid to this important topic. Professional lighting includes spotlights, uplights, the use of gels, even changing the overall ambient lighting in a room. But a lighting technician is no mind reader — it is important to be clear as to what kind of lighting you'd like and in what color scheme.

Candlelight

Candlelight is one of the most wonderful ways to transform the mood in a room. Perhaps the popularity of the warm glow of candles is due to the fact that candlelight flatters everyone. Candles create a romantic, magical mood. Flickering candles remind one of the twinkling of starlight, but there's a warmth to them as well, evoking the age-old associations of fire with life-affirming heat, hearth, home, and protection. And, of course, candles are spiritual. As wonderful as they are, be aware that lighting a room just with candles causes whites to appear whiter and darks darker. A room's details are apt to disappear when lit by candlelight alone. If you want this effect, use as much white as possible and avoid deeply colored florals or other decor details. A very simple design is to literally line the room with candles, putting them all along the walls and in every corner. It's a wonderful effect.

Candles come in three main forms: votive, pillar, and taper. Votives, in particular, throw off a different type of light. This is due in part to the fact that they are often placed below eye level, on tables or consoles, so that the light they give is usually an uplight, that is, illuminating from below. Votives provide an intimate kind of lighting, but owing to their size, the light they give is less for illumination than for show. Tapers and pillars, on the other hand, are by their very nature raised. Thus, they are often used to provide more-ambient light or simply to draw the eye upward.

Votives are fabulous because they come in such an incredible variety and selection. You can tailor them to any theme, color scheme, or mood. Generally, votives are used in groupings, and it is my feeling that the more the merrier. There are so many different varieties: plain glass, such as those used in churches; rimmed in metals like silver, brass or gold; different colored glass, including the lovely cobalt blue. Votives come square or round — the selection is endless. If you are doing

Lighting for a Wedding Aisle

Here is an interesting comparison: two different lighting effects for two entirely different wedding-aisle decors. In fact, these two events were even held in the same space at the Pierre Hotel in New York. First, on page 52, we have a spring wedding, complete with cherry blossom branches in oversize containers forming the archway over the aisle. And hanging from the branches were simple white votive candles, providing the warm glow of candlelight suspended as if in time. The combination of the translucent blossoms lit by the floating candles made for a most romantic ambience in which to be married. The mirror at the back of the room even cooperated by multiplying and reflecting back the candlelight to the viewer.

In the second example of wedding-aisle lighting, tapers were used along the aisle instead of votives. The overhead lighting was kept quite dim, making the uplighting of the archway and arrangements that much more dramatic. Large, tree-size candelabras lavishly decorated with primrose, grapes, lilacs, and viburnum were placed along the aisle, each with an assortment of electric taper candles topped with miniature lampshades. The result is similar to the previous example in the sense that the candlelight is placed high enough that it seems to float. But the different candles and decorations used created a significantly different mood in each case. This was a fall wedding, designed to remind guests of the happy time of the harvest and Sukkoth.

something with a contemporary sensibility, use modern-looking votives such as frosted white. If you are doing something traditional, use votives that have a traditional finish such as gilded silver. And don't worry about how long they will stay lit. Most votives last twelve hours, which is more than enough time for any event. If you light them early, before it grows dark, their glow will make a nice transition through dusk. They are also cost-effective, so you can use as many as you want. While some public spaces have guidelines about open fires, most places allow them.

Pillar candles give more of an impression of solidity, perhaps even solemnity. Usually tall, these substantial candles are most often round but can also be square or rectangular. Placed on tables, buffets, and consoles, they add weight. Votives may be more intimate, but pillars make a greater design statement. For one thing they are bigger, and people really like the sturdiness of them. Pairing them with votives can be quite nice.

Tapers come in a variety of lengths, but the longer the better. Traditional tapers are generally associated with the most elegant of events. The length and slimness of tapers means that the ideal effect is to raise them up as if it were their very nature to reach to the heavens. It is also a good way to create the illusion of height in a room, or even to break up space in a room with high ceilings. The candles will draw the eye upward. For example, placing twenty-four-inch tapers on holders quite high in a room that is dimly lit causes the candlelight to appear as though it were floating in the air.

Tall tapers can cause problems if the melting wax drips. Most venues are either air-conditioned or heated, or even outdoors, and are thus prone to be drafty. The slightest breeze can cause tapers to spray wax. Candle wax dripped all over the glassware is an unsightly problem. However, someone was clever enough to invent a candle that appears to be a classic taper but is actually a taper within a follower that surrounds the candle and prevents any spillage of wax. These are not that expensive,

Something Different with a Traditional Lampshade

For this wedding reception we created a three-armed sculptural centerpiece encased by red roses, amaranthus, red berries, and hydrangeas. The venue, Cipriani 42nd Street in New York, is fantastically spacious, but its high ceilings require appropriately proportioned decorations. On this occasion we created a design that both fit the space and was an unusual lighting effect as well. Pillar candles proved perfect for the purpose. We created a magnificent triune centerpiece, nearly overburdened it with roses and berries, then created a "lamp" on each arm. Using pillar candles as the light source, we topped the arrangement with classic lampshades. As icing on the cake, we threw some tulle over the shades for a bit of whimsy and shimmer. Voila! An original way to approach an especially lofty and spacious venue.

Lotus Lighting Centerpieces at a Valentine's Day Party

Inspired lighting gave this Valentine's Day party a new twist. Centerpieces fashioned from silk and wire were lit from within with votives, creating what appeared to be a lovely lotus blossom on every table. The lotus, long important in Asian spirituality and symbolism, is lunar in aspect, suggesting the mystery and magic of the moon. Lunar symbolism was evident elsewhere in the room — in the glistening silver organza overlays that bedecked the tables and the cool white lighting that illuminated the room. The turning of the lotus is said to represent creativity and its watery nature is an aspect of the feminine, watery associations of the moon. It also symbolizes fertility and compassion, the highest form of love. What could be better to light a party celebrating love! Wide open, the flowers beckon and exude a romantic glow. Additional blossoms on curved aluminum stems suggest movement, reaching playfully upward to provide a fanciful accompaniment to the main flower. Gardenias at every place setting echoed the lotus shape.

To create an atmosphere of romance, the room was dimly lit. Architectural details in the white columns were uplighted to provide drama and effect. In keeping with common practice, the sides of the room were lit, as were the decorative screens placed there. Festooned with garlands of ruby red roses and boxwood, the screens framed oversize heart-shaped rose-covered wreaths — the more traditional symbol of the day.

many florists carry them, and they solve the problem. If open flame is a concern, there are pillars available that are electric or battery operated.

I don't usually place too many candles on buffets and consoles, unless I have a specific effect in mind. These areas have a utilitarian purpose and as such require some elbowroom on the part of guests. Moreover, since food or other items are placed there, it's best to give these areas good illumination, with spotlights, for example, to enable guests to see what they are doing and to highlight the artistry of the food.

How to transform existing lighting

In most ballrooms or public venues, the basic ambient lighting is all on dimmers, so you are able to control the intensity of the light and thus the overall mood of the room to suit your vision. Lighting that is lower or dimmer is more intimate or romantic. Somewhat brighter lighting tends to be more businesslike. Of course, with tents a lighting engineer is required and so you have complete control over the lighting. In a home or other types of venues such as restaurants, you also have some control in the sense that you can exchange existing lightbulbs for brighter or softer ones, even unscrew them completely, or replace them with colored ones if you wish.

Aside from working with a venue's ambient lighting, the most basic way of lighting a room is to go to all the corners and uplight them. This gives the room dimension and character. Do the same for any architectural or decorative details you'd like to have stand out. Uplighting is created when you place the lighting fixtures on the floor and the illumination goes upward. So that's the first thing you should do when lighting a room. Second, there are many different ways to spotlight the areas where you need more light, such as the dining tables and the buffet. In spotlighting the fixture hangs down from above and directs a specific beam of illumination on a certain object. Usually one spotlight is not enough for large arrangements or other areas; three spots directed at the same thing works best. For the ceremony portion of a wedding celebration, it is best to spotlight the bridal couple, almost theatrically, in order to ensure that they are the center of attention and so that each guest can truly see the ceremony.

There are rules about flowers and lighting. Remember that at night, whites do not tend to need much lighting, while darker-hued flowers need extra help, otherwise they will fade into the background. It's important to enhance dark flowers by lighting so you can see them better. As colors go brighter or as illumination is increased, there is a general shift toward yellow, while if colors are deeper or illumination is decreased, color will tend toward violet. The best way to create luster is to produce an overall impression of subdued light.

When I want an effect that the lighting infrastructure of a venue can't provide or when I use a tent for an event, I work with a lighting technician, who then provides and installs lighting fixtures. It's best to make sure lighting fixtures are as small and unobstrusive as possible. Lighting is necessary but you want to downplay it. I have learned that fixtures are fixtures. There's no point in trying to hide what they are at an event. Just as the lamp in your home may be an attractive ornament, it still serves mainly a utilitarian function and is still a lamp. You can't very well hide it. Fixtures are not hidden in the theater either. They are painted black so they fade into the background. I advocate this approach at my events. It's important to have the fixtures blend into a room (if the room is all white, obviously the fixtures should be too). Trying to disguise fixtures with ribbons or draping only draws attention to them.

Most lighting designers will use gels — heat-tolerant plastic — to insert into or cover their lighting fixtures. This allows them to vary the color or intensity of the lighting. A good lighting designer knows to intensify the illumination at the ceiling but keep the intensity lower at the level where people are to be gathered. No one looks good in the glare of lighting that is too intense.

Lighting Evokes Loftier Ideas

Subdued ambient lighting used in conjunction with spotlights and pillar candles conveyed just the right solemnity of purpose at this event for Meals on Wheels, also shown earlier. Spotlights on the room's support columns drew the eye upward and made the space interesting. Meanwhile, the tapers and votives on the table glowed behind a screen, giving a starlike effect.

Using lighting to create mood

Working with colored lighting is a wonderful way to create a mood and to bring out the best in your decorations. Using a magenta gel to spotlight an arrangement of deep reds and burgundys will deepen and enhance the colors in the flowers, making them seem even more vibrant.

Color truly affects the energy of a space. Magenta is a very flattering color to everyone. Much like the warm golden hues of candlelight, it works well with all skin tones. I am especially fond of using the warmth of orange to evoke a sense of dusk or sundown, that enchanting time of transformation from day to night. Blue is useful mainly as an effect. Blue lighting can be exotic and exciting, but you have to be careful not to overdo it, since it has a tendency to make everyone look like a Martian. That goes double for green.

I've found that when lighting a dance floor, the most important thing is to bring up the energy. Make the lighting brighter or more intense and spot the floor with a myriad of colors, just like at a nightclub or discotheque. I like a variety of blinking red, blue, yellow, and green lights. This can be set up quite easily and seems to jazz people up and encourage them to move with abandon.

There are many ways of enhancing a room with colored lighting. One is intelligent lighting: fixtures that are set on timers so that the lighting changes color and intensity several times during the course of an evening according to a prescribed plan. One of my favorite schemes is this: Just as guests arrive, the lighting is dawn or sunset colored, with plenty of gold. This is a warm, inviting color scheme for cocktails and perfect for relaxing into the tenor of the event, much like sitting on the beach just around sundown in the late summer. Next the lighting switches to magenta for the dinner period, working with the candlelight and bathing guests in a flattering and atmospheric glow. Later on, for dancing, when the party increases in energy, you change the lighting again. Intelligent lighting is a wonderful way of creating a mood and

A Corporate Event to Accentuate the Positive

When I met with the representatives of the business firm sponsoring this event, they told me they wanted an elegant affair that would communicate to its guests both the company's successes and its hopes for the future. To accommodate the six hundred people who were to attend, we raised a large tent with an unusually high ceiling and then built an internal structure over the dance floor to break up the space for warmth. The beauty of the blank canvas of a tent is that it acts perfectly as a screen for projection. Capitalizing on this happy circumstance, we unobtrusively placed slide projectors all around the room and projected images of blue sky with fluffy billowing clouds all over the ceiling. What better way to say, "The sky's the limit"? Notice the twenty-four-inch taper candles on elongated stands set on each table, drawing the eye upward and again implying lofty goals. Black tablecloths allowed the lighting to be the star of this event. The lighting technician bathed the room in a warm glow of magenta, the most flattering color for human skin, making guests appear unusually soft and good looking and adding an overall warmth and sense of well-being to the room. Completing the overall statement of success and goals achieved were monumental floral victory wreaths placed along the sides of the room.

then controlling it very subtly without attracting the guests' awareness. Using it is a little like being the Wizard of Oz. For Joan Rivers's daughter Melissa's wedding, lighting designer Bentley Meeker actually used intelligent lighting to simulate the northern lights. Throughout the ceremony, the light subtly moved and changed, much as the aurora borealis does in the northern sky.

As for other types of lighting, personally, I am not fond of Christmas lights because I think they are overused. I mean the small white electric lights that come in strands. These are often used to great effect to create a kind of sparkling or magical feeling, and they are inexpensive. But nowadays they are often the first thing anyone turns to, and yet there are other ways to create a similar effect, for instance, with hanging candles. There are a number of ways to hang votives and the effect is much more magical than that of Christmas lights. Another way is to use extraordinarily tall tapers. For Christmas, what I like to do is use the larger, old-fashioned bulbs in green and red. There's something about them that is very homey and reminds people of yesteryear. Those small twinkle lights did not exist when many of us were kids.

There are also many different types of hanging lanterns. These, of course, must be illuminated electrically. A multitude of hanging paper lanterns can be enchanting. Annette Roque used them for her wedding to Matt Lauer. The effect was marvelous. For outdoors, consider torches. Put torches around the swimming pool or line the walkway to a tent with them. There are torches and lanterns of many kinds.

Nontraditional lighting effects

A lighting effect that has worked well for a number of the events I've designed is the use of projection. You project any imagery that you want on a wall, ceiling, or other surface from either the front or the back. It's a bit theatrical. Rear projection, in particular, is relatively new and isn't often done, so it makes a bit of a statement at an event. I've found

An Illuminated Wedding Aisle

The classical architecture and graceful formality of the Terrace Room of the Plaza Hotel is ideally suited to such a solemn occasion as a wedding ceremony; however, any multipurpose space requires some reconfiguring. In this case, to set the scene for the wedding, we first uplit the gorgeous arches in the room, thereby making the ceiling of the space as lofty as that of a religious site. Then, to clarify the wedding aisle, we constructed the lighting fixtures shown. Appearing to be lamp shades with varying circumferences and lengths, these lightweight shades were covered in dendrobium orchids. Within the shades were light fixtures triggered by movement sensors. As the bridal procession moved down the aisle, the lights came on so that, ultimately, when the bride made her way down the aisle, she walked on a carpet of white light — a highly dramatic and unusual effect.

that it works especially well with tents, since the canvas acts perfectly as a blank screen. Keep in mind that you need at least ten feet between the projector and the screen in order for the image to be seen.

You can project any type of image that you'd like. Family photographs, images of architectural details, a photograph of a garden, a river, a sky. For example, if you project beautiful garden images onto the walls of a tent, the feeling within becomes one of being in the outdoors. You can get the images from photographic stock houses. Whatever image works with your event or color scheme can be rented or purchased. Or you can shoot whatever you want — make your own pictures.

Lighting and lighting effects can be among the most wonderful ways to express yourself by highlighting your concept and creating a mood. Don't cheat yourself by neglecting the lighting. Instead, view it as a wonderful opportunity to be even more artistic or creative.

Using Rear Projection for a Wedding Altar

The task here was to create an unusual setting for a wedding altar, which was to be on a stage. My clients wanted a simple setting for their traditional wedding canopy, the chuppah. We decided to give the altar the feeling of being in nature by projecting an image of a lush garden as a backdrop to the event. The chuppah, fashioned from a cream-colored fabric hand painted in a gently romantic floral motif, and the unobtrusive arrangements of cherry blossoms flanking it worked in perfect harmony with the backdrop. In a simple, nearly humble way, the entire effect is created by the projection. The result is a setting that is rich, theatrical, and most unusual, yet one of momentousness and joy.

Chapter 4

Working with Space

HOW TO TRANSFORM A ROOM

Once there is a design concept for an event, including a sense of the desired mood, degree of texture, and lighting, it is time to deal with the realities of space. No matter what kind of party you are planning, one of your most important decisions will be the venue you choose for it. Naturally, a significant part of your decision making will relate to the scale of your event: how many guests you plan to invite and how you intend to entertain them. For example, if you are planning a traditional wedding, you may require a ceremony area, a cocktail area, and an area for a sit-down dinner. Or perhaps you are hosting a cocktail party, where the majority of guests will be standing. Practical issues such as these will, in large part, determine your venue.

But the choice of any venue comes with constraints. The availability of appropriate rooms at hotels or restaurants may be limited, tents and public facilities have their drawbacks, and even working in your own home can pose problems. It will come as no surprise that the greater the degree of control you wish to have over every detail of the occasion, the greater the expense will be. Generally, anything can be rented, so if you truly know exactly what you want, then lease it. This often means building an entire venue from scratch—usually by raising a tent. But no location is perfect. The challenge is in adapting the setting to your vision, despite any obstacles that may come along. This is part of the creative process, and in fact, problem solving can lead to quite a few inventive solutions that contribute to your vision in ways you may never have even thought about!

A few points about venue choice

Simply because it is more intimate, many people would choose to hold an event at home but are unable to because they are limited by the amount of space available. Thus, you have to seek out what venues are available for lease. Most fine hotels have ballrooms and other accommodations designed to house events. Often restaurants also have special rooms for larger-scale parties. The advantage of both these options is that they usually come with all the necessary amenities — from tablecloths and linens to cooking facilities and catering staff. This saves you from worry about further rental.

Rarely is any situation perfect. There are drawbacks to using hotels and restaurants. You might want more control over the food, linen, and tableware, for example, than these venues allow. Also, the decor of these places often leaves something to be desired. Though the room may be decorated in a lovely neoclassical style, this may not fit with the type of party you'd like to give. In addition, especially in smaller cities, people may have seen that particular location many times before. All of these factors point to one conclusion: It is well worth personalizing the decor of the venue you choose to suit your own style.

Many people think that there isn't much one can do to personalize a public space. This is hardly the case. With a little ingenuity, anything is possible. Just empower yourself by overcoming any rigidity in your thinking. Using a little imagination, you can apply your vision to any space. Think of the room as a blank canvas and go to work. See any constraints that you might encounter, such as architectural features, preexisting decor, or other details, as opportunities to think creatively. I've

A Classic White-and-Pastel Wedding Reception Infused with a Sense of Whimsy

This is one of three events we show for comparison — held at the Pierre Hotel's main ballroom. This wedding reception (also shown on page 68) was based around the classic color palette for romance: whites and creams mixed with pastels, contributing to a mood of joyful promise and hope. We created lush floral arrangements to fill the space intersecting the center of the room. The arrangements did this in two ways: by rising up from the tables and also by hanging down from the ceiling.

The ivory paper-and-wire decorations are Venetian in inspiration and are vaguely reminiscent of paper sculptures hung upside down. Laden with vibernum, roses, pale green hydrangeas, and hanging amaranthus, they were oddly compelling and generated just enough whimsy to be fun. They not only lowered the ceiling to enhance the intimacy of the space but also fit with the event's pastel color scheme and brightened the room, since they were lit from within. The florals in the centerpieces bubbled upward and outward from clear crystal raised vases, which echoed the room's crystal chandeliers. Even those were bedecked in blooms.

In addition, we covered all the existing drapery with white swaths of extra-wide fabric to keep the overall room in line with the concept. Keeping the main color in the white family, we used table overlays of white-dotted raw silk. Each place setting held a neatly folded white linen napkin into which was tucked a single cream-colored rose. The gold organza seat covers affixed with white satin ribbons were the perfect complement to the beaded gold chargers. A once ordinary room was transformed into a statement of elegance, romance, and grace.

A Fairyland

For another occasion at the Pierre, we were
inspired to create an imaginative fairy tale
world, one that would have been fit for a
scene in Shakespeare's romantic comedy
A Midsummer Night's Dream. Again, we
created an elaborate ceiling effect. Here a
grid was built across the ceiling, decorated
with wisteria and an array of roses in a
rich profusion of colors. Then we projected
the image of a starry sky behind it. Large-
scale topiaries rising from neoclassical
urns were set on each table. Every other
topiary also held a delightful crystal candelabra that perfectly matched the room's
chandeliers. If the chandeliers didn't reveal
otherwise, you'd hardly guess it was the
same room shown in the previous photograph. In fact, you might even believe that
the setting was actually a lyrical fairy garden
deep in the most lush part of summer —
an environment fit for Oberon and Titania.

Repapering the Walls

The third and perhaps most dramatic transformation we achieved at the Pierre was for a wedding. The client did not want the room's traditional-looking decor, so the challenge was to convert a traditional room into something different or unusual. Since the client had spent part of her childhood in Japan, she hoped to make the backdrop of the event reflect the simplicity of traditional Japanese design. So, taking a Japanese shoji screen as our inspiration, we literally covered over the room. We used rice paper to cover all the more ornate "traditional" elements of the space such as drapes and woodwork and held the paper in place with slats of wood, to complete the shojilike effect. If you look carefully at these two photographs you'll notice the balustrade at the perimeter of the room that has been entirely masked here. Exuberant floral arrangements in a palette of whites, purples, pale lavenders, and just the hint of pink provided the primary color for the reception. The delicately lovely design of the seat covers was hand painted on smoky gray silk. Silvery taupe overlays with just a hint of embroidery and the simplicity of the seat covers kept the lines of the room clean. The overall result was quiet, almost meditative, yet glamorous.

often found that constraints give rise to some of the most interesting decor details. But no matter what the design issue you encounter, it is key to match the scale of the decor elements to the scale of the room.

Most rooms are rented for their capacity, but frequently a room is a bit too large for the number of people attending or has elements such as an extremely high ceiling that enlarge it psychologically. On the whole, I've found people like a sense of spaciousness or a feeling of openness. It makes them feel more comfortable. I have done parties for two hundred people in rooms that fit five hundred. It's preferable, in fact, to have too much capacity rather than too little simply because there are many ways to correct it. However, it's important in such a situation that the space doesn't feel overwhelming or empty and cold to your guests. Don't try to fill the space by spreading tables around the room. Rather, group tables together to foster intimacy, leaving space at the edges of the room. You can also erect screens or partitions to break up the venue or encircle guests, making the room feel smaller. Ceilings that are extremely high can be good because one gets a sense of loftiness of purpose not unlike in a house of worship. However, for interest, the overhead space needs to be dealt with or pierced in some manner. For example, hang decorative elements, create canopies, or even build arbors or false ceilings. Above all, do not leave large amounts of space to drain off into darkness; keep the room well lit in order to keep it feeling warm.

However, if the opposite occurs and the room you've hired is a bit tight for the number of guests, be more sparing in the decor. Too much could make the room feel cramped or claustrophobic. Your aim should be to open up the room. Use airy or minimalist decorations. Create a strong focal point at the center of the space and be sure to light the walls and corners brightly to enlarge the room visually. In the same vein, spotlight low ceilings. You might consider providing a buffet rather than a sit-down dinner. You also want to take care where you place the waiters' stations, buffets, and consoles, keeping in mind that traffic flow is hampered in a smaller space.

Another category of venue is the public museum, garden, conservatory, private club, or historic mansion. These are places that are not ordinarily in the event business. However, many have opened their doors in exchange for fees or donations. Such unexpected locations allow for a more unusual or memorable experience. Few forget an event held at the spectacularly impressive Temple of Dendur at New York's Metropolitan Museum. The added benefit of these venues is that sometimes an event can be held in conjunction with a special exhibit, thus permitting guests to linger after hours at a facility to enjoy an exhibit in private. I have structured events at the Pierpont Morgan Library in New York, for example, where guests not only enjoyed a party but were also given access to exhibits of rare books and manuscripts. As for weddings, keep in mind that some public facilities are not permitted to host religious ceremonies.

Remember that these types of venue may have special design issues or limited amenities. As wonderful as the architecture of such spaces may be, it is often highly unique and therefore it will be a greater challenge to effect a personal statement in them. Events there can also be more expensive to produce, since you may have to rent anything from the silverware to the tables. One potential positive to this sort of arrangement is that you are free to select the caterer of your choice rather than use the food and beverage facilities in place at hotels and restaurants. So if you are particular about the type or quality of the food served, you are able to have more control. All of these conditions also apply to using a tent for your venue. Depending on your electrical needs, sometimes with tents the available power is insufficient and a generator is necessary. In that case, a backup generator is always a good idea. Everything you need is usually available from the firm that leases the tent.

Though it may sound surprising, for me, tents are the most desirable venues for an event. I like the feeling of tents and the freedom in working with them. They are big open spaces, like blank canvases. Tents also give you the flexibility of location, since they can be raised anywhere.

A Reception with an Open-Air Feel

The aim for the decor of this wedding reception was that it give the feeling of being in the open air while also conveying a sense of elegance. Disney executive Robert Iger and television anchor Willow Bay wanted their reception to feel as natural and as much a part of the outdoors as possible but also to be a little different. So they selected clear walls for the tent, which was raised on a property in the Hamptons. We built an arbor with two purposes in mind. The first was to enhance the feeling of truly being outdoors and the second was to minimize the sense of being in a tent by masking its supports, which were covered with grapevine and ivy. Then we hung additional grapevines down to the center of each table to serve as a kind of trellis for brightly colored florals in pinks and reds. Each table seemed to have its own unusual variety of climbing and flowering plant all to itself.

So many of my clients would really love to hold their events outdoors, but because of concerns about such weather as rain or excessive heat, or because of other considerations such as pests, they don't dare. So the next best thing is to hold the event outside using a tent and then to create a decor that reflects the beauty of nature as closely as possible. As can be seen, the clear walls of the tent extend the line of vision, making the room seem very spacious and open. Together with the vine-covered arbor and the brightly colored flower arrangements, the aim of a natural feel in the room was achieved in a rather simple yet elegant way.

Turning a Tent into a Ballroom

As first glance, you wouldn't think this decor is within a tent, would you? It could easily be mistaken for a ballroom. That's exactly the effect we wanted! My client preferred the flexibility of a tent for this occasion but wanted to eat her cake too, so to speak. The greatest challenge for us was how to approach the tent's ceiling so it would have the height and detail of a ballroom's ceiling. So in a bit of sleight of hand, we photographed elements of traditional ballroom decor and printed them on giant panels of fabric. The sections of fabric were then sewn together to create an entire tableau and stretched across a frame, which was suspended from the roof of the tent, giving the event the feel of a traditional room. The fabric is important. We like to print on fabrics that are sturdy but with a translucency to them. This way we can work with lighting the piece from above or below. The second issue we had to deal with was the walls. What does a ballroom wall look like? We used the same technique to produce the screens that lined the room. Notice we even created what looks like a parquet dance floor. Presto! A venue as impressive as any found in the finest hotels.

A Garden Pavilion

Tents come in so many shapes and varieties today. Some have no walls at all, for that feeling of really being in the open air. Others have walls or ceilings of clear plastic. I don't recommend using these during the day, since they can definitely create a "greenhouse" effect if it is sunny and warm, causing flowers — and guests — to wilt. A nighttime event is another situation altogether, since it can be romantic to look outdoors or even up at the stars on a clear night. Another option is to use a tent with plastic windows set into the sides. You might want to request this. This allows you to look outside without being subjected to the vagaries of weather.

The tent shown here was for an event at Wave Hill, a spectacular public garden and cultural center overlooking the Hudson River in the Bronx, New York. Because the setting was so stunning, the host and hostess requested windows for the tent. This gave rise to the idea of decorating the tent to look like a garden pavilion. We built a bower made of birch branches and covered it with grapevine and dripping moss and uplighted it with spotlights. Though rustic, the room also reflected the rich abundance of Mother Nature with luxuriant floral arrangements dripping with fresh crimson berries and sumptuous fabrics in deep reds. With the smallest whisper of inspiration from the Petit Trianon and the gardens of Versailles, the venue became worthy of Marie Antoinette.

Draping a Tent for Specific Effect

When the new tower annex to the Guggenheim Museum in New York was completed, the museum held an opening celebration. The dinner was to be held in a tent raised in a garden across the street from the museum. The Guggenheim's distinctive curvilinear and organic architecture by Frank Lloyd Wright proved to be the inspiration for the tent's decor. This is an example of draping put to unusually successful use. All the draping in the tent mirrored the rounded lines of the museum building with great sweeps of fabric reined in by an elaborate system of cables and wires. We even hid the tent poles with draping. In keeping with the color of the Guggenheim, everything was white, the linens, the flowers — even the floor was painted white. The effect was as sculptural as the museum itself.

Often they are the ideal compromise when you'd like to have a party at your home for sentimental reasons but simply don't have the space. Pitch a tent on your own property and it's the best of both worlds.

Another reason people use tents is because they want that special ambience of an event in the open air, but concern for the vagaries of weather means a tent is prudent. Tents can be air-conditioned and heated. And if you choose a tent with walls that open up and the day's weather proves to be perfect, you can create an open-air feeling by throwing back the tent's walls. Of course, if need be, the walls can be kept lowered to provide shelter from wind and rain.

My clients approach tents in a variety of ways. Some people like all that white canvas and some choose to transform it completely. You can let the tent interior be one large space or even create rooms within the room or put in sufficient structures so that it feels like a room in a building or your home. One thing to consider when using a tent is flooring. Many people raise a tent over a tennis court because it provides an existing floor. We've even literally painted over the court with a design to create a dance floor. Of course, afterward it goes back to its original form. Other times, I've created a wooden floor over which we raised a tent.

Flow — moving people around your party

No matter where you hold your party, one thing to keep in mind is the flow of your event. By *flow* I mean how your guests will move around. Allowing some movement is always good because otherwise your guests may feel cooped up or bored and become restless. Remember, the idea is for guests to be relaxed and comfortable. So arrange for them to move around a bit, to circulate. This keeps the energy of your event alive rather than stagnant. At the same time, you have to work to keep guests together in tight groupings for the sake of social interaction and intimacy. If there is too much space or if the flow is not well planned,

Transmuting a Room into an Art Deco Smoking Lounge

In a startling example of before and after, I've provided an image of an anteroom at the St. Regis Hotel in New York. This room could be used for any number of purposes, but in this case we decided to give it a makeover. By redraping the windows, importing some new furniture, and incorporating a few choice decorations, we turned the room into an art deco smoking lounge to be enjoyed late in the evening following dinner. Something as simple as the removal of the existing drapes produced quite a change in the room's overall appearance. So did uplighting the walls and details of the room. It immediately created another look altogether, one that is much cleaner and more contemporary. One of the key "tricks" in this instance, however, was covering over the existing carpet by bringing in an entirely new floor of black and white vinyl squares.

Though the room was available, my client could have chosen not to use it at all, given that its decor was more traditional than the event. But she wanted to give the event some flow, so we decided that it would be worth refreshing the space. In the end, it was all worthwhile, since quite a few guests enjoyed the area later in the evening.

A Roman-Theme Tent Decor

The host of this event wanted a dramatic decor that took elements from ancient Rome. First we concentrated on the entrance. We wanted to build an entrance that was serious enough to give a hint of the drama to come but also rather playful. We built an actual archway through which to enter the main dining room and placed an ornate gold classical embellishment above it. Then, in keeping with the marble architecture of the Romans, we framed the entranceway with white fabric columns printed with decorative gold detailing that were lit from within. The columns were an interesting design element — one used in the main dining area too — since they were at once attractive and a bit tongue-in-cheek.

Often when we work in a tent, we put down a wooden floor. But in this case we painted over the floor of the tennis court on which the tent had been raised. As the client did not mind, we hand painted the dance floor in the center of the room. (Believe it or not, this is less expensive than putting down a wooden floor, and the client can just redo the court after the party.)

In keeping with the idea of Roman marble, in the main room we left the tent's white ceiling bare but draped the sides with white gauze to soften the look. We also hung gold-fringed draping at various points for drama. A final touch to this Roman-inspired space was the projection of images of classical Roman architecture along the walls.

guests may scatter, making your party seem a little empty. Controlling the flow of a party requires a delicate balance. You want to encourage or control some movement, but you don't want people to feel herded or moved around too much, since this will disrupt their sense of comfort.

When your guests first arrive at an event, perhaps they will be ushered into one area for cocktails, or if at a wedding, to the area where the ceremony will take place. Or if you wish, you might have them linger at the entranceway to your event or in the area where you have your escort table. This could serve as a transition space — the place where guests throw off their day, the stresses they've brought with them, and begin to get into the spirit of the event. Serving cocktails accompanied by relaxing music is ideal for this.

Next guests may move to the dining area for the main meal. Dessert may be served elsewhere, but few of my clients choose this option, unless they are entertaining in their own homes, since the convenience of the tables makes it more practical to serve dessert there. Another way to shift the energy of an event is by clearing the tables and beginning the dancing. Here, as discussed in the previous chapter, lighting is key. Shifting the lighting to something more atmospheric or energetic will encourage flow. Ideally, at this point guests will be inspired to get up and dance or even simply to stretch their legs, move around a bit, and mingle.

When entertaining at home, you might have drinks in the garden or by the swimming pool, dinner in the dining area or perhaps even under a tent outside, and dessert served in the living quarters. As for tents, depending on the location and how big the property is, it's best to have one tent for the ceremony, one for cocktails — this is in a perfect world — and a third tent for the reception. The caterers may even need a smaller tent for the kitchen. This keeps people together while changing the environment for them.

Something else I've done at parties is create a sitting area for guests to move to if they want a quieter, more comfortable, or intimate environment. If you're in the middle of the party and there's too much noise or music, you can always go to the sitting area and find people to socialize with. A note of caution, however: If your sitting area is too large or appealing, there's the danger that your event will become split, as though you had two separate parties. When an event consists of a couple of hundred people and half of them are congregated in the sitting room, the energy of the party changes.

Another point is that at a wedding reception or a dinner hosted to celebrate someone, it's important to create an area or areas where the guest of honor or the bride and groom will be accessible to the guests. For example, arrange a situation where they can welcome people formally. Or place them in the most accessible part of the dining area. This is usually in front of the dance floor or closest to the most central part of the room. The important thing is to allow the guests to see or visit this area.

So when designing the decor of your event, remember to consider flow. Often the scale of a room or tent is large enough to permit breaking up the space into smaller functional areas that enable you to control flow. This is accomplished through the creative use of boundaries or screens. Another way to control flow is the table arrangement. Table groupings create separate areas. Also the placement of consoles, buffets, and bar areas is important, in two ways: First, the physical boundaries they create as objects force people to move around them, enabling you to control the flow or movement of people. Second, they are important because tables attract people. Like bees to honey, guests will group around hors d'oeuvres, bar areas, and buffets, so placement of them is a way to encourage congregation as well as to get people to go where you want them to go.

Transforming a room

Once you have the architecture of your space and a sense of how you want to break up that space, it's time to consider how you want to trans-

Psyche and Eros Celebrate Love

The unusual classical gold statuettes we used as centerpieces gave this anniversary celebration a bit of drama. They are made of plaster and are available for purchase, and we were inspired to cover them with gold leaf to spectacular results. The statuettes sat on a bed of crimson, magenta, and pink roses — all the colors of love. Draping enlivened the tent space, and its gold detailing matched the table ornaments as well as the gold chairs. Images of the pink blossoms of springtime in all their bright promise reflected off the walls. Sumptuous Chinese red table linens and a dance floor painted to match announced that passion and a love of life were being celebrated in high style.

form the room to reflect your vision. Remember that anything is possible. A room can be completely transformed even though you are on a budget. Just keep your focus on what you want, your vision. Whether you want to change an existing room in a hotel, for example, simply because it is dull or there are aspects to it that need camouflaging, or want to build a space from scratch in a tent, all you need is a little ingenuity.

Realizing that anything can be added or hidden, consider the use of screens and other boundaries such as foliage, platforms, fabric, or new carpeting, or even putting down a new floor to achieve your design. Fabric can work miracles. Hang, drape, and swag your way into a new room. Flair is what is important here, and flair can be stymied by preconceived notions of what can't be done.

To give you an example of how completely a room can be transformed, in this chapter I've included three events that all took place in the main ballroom at the Pierre Hotel. You would hardly think it is the same room. The only things that belie this are the light fixtures. In two instances we created a new format for the ceiling. In another we completely transformed the walls. In an amusing twist, not only have we transformed traditional venues such as ballrooms to look like something else, but I've also transformed a tent to look like a ballroom! Perhaps by seeing what can be achieved with a little ingenuity, you will be inspired to view any venue for your events a bit differently — not as a static given but more as a backdrop with all the potential in the world to help you effect your vision.

Chapter 5

DESIGNING THE DETAILS

Your success in executing a vision for your event depends in large part on the many decisions made about all the details surrounding it. Meticulous attention to detail is the difference between a ho-hum soiree and a fabulous evening. It is all the little well-attended details acting in concert that best represent your ideas. Your vision is the conversation, but the details are your vocabulary. Ignoring the importance of each small decision or, worse, caring so little that you allow these decisions to be made in the usual or obvious way can spell disaster in terms of the overall energy, comfort, and happiness of your guests. Imaginative planning and attention to detail make your event unique.

My advice to any party giver is to *think*. Think about what you want, how something will fit into your concept, and whether what is traditional is really best. Question everything. Do not rest on platitudes. Look at every choice and decision from a fresh point of view. While you may have engaged any number of professionals to help you with various aspects of your event — from florists to caterers — do not leave anything to chance. Keep an eye on the details and make all the decisions yourself rather than have them made for you by default. This will ensure the fulfillment of your unique vision.

Working alone, you might find yourself harried. I can't impress on you more strongly how much happier you'll be with the end result if you take the time to simply meditate on each small issue as it comes up. Which fabric suits you best? Does the menu fit in with the overall theme? What kind of chairs do you want to use? Should they be covered or left bare? How do you use buffets and consoles to promote your decor? What do you do about hallways or entranceways in order to maximize the welcome your guests will receive? These are just a few of the questions thinking about your many decisions and choices will elicit. This idea of taking a fresh approach applies to all the details of your affair, including those involving the food, wine, service arrangements, even your clothing, but all of these are beyond the scope of this book.

Entrance and escort arrangements that command attention

The entrance area is the first thing your guests see when they arrive at an event. It gives a clear message of what is to come. If you are creative about this one aspect of your event, you will be communicating that what's in store for your guests is no ordinary party. It's a good way to get their attention immediately. Let them think, "This is kind of interesting—if this is special, what's the rest of the night going to be like?" Thus, the escort table becomes important as a statement. Do you want a traditional table with a small floral arrangement and classic place cards? Or do you want to do something different? Think of ways you can make it more original. Depending on your central idea, take certain liberties. You could hang place cards on strings and tie them to an arbor of flowers. Alternatively, you could fashion unique place cards out of unusual materials such as metal or plastic, even handmade paper. Or emboss or print place cards with symbols that are meaningful to you. I can't stress enough that if you give it a little thought, it doesn't have to be done in any way but your own.

◄ A Perfect Rhapsody in Pink

The exacting eye and heart of the hostess for this event demanded perfection right down to the last detail (page 92). The result is an escort-card table that is a study in taste, style, and the harmonious combination of elements. A bonanza of bursting peonies massed together makes for a cotton candy delight as guests arrive. Such a simple grouping of blossoms in a most refined clear crystal vase immediately evoked what the hostess wanted to achieve at the event: a soft, feminine romanticism. The arrangement anchors the center of the table. The place cards radiate outward from it in streaming rays of white that signify energy and movement. Each card was coupled with a dendrobium orchid blossom in the same blushing tone of pink as the peonies. We chose a beautiful pink beaded tablecloth as the backdrop for the perfect lines of this design. Notice the careful thought that even went into the shape of the cards. Each was folded in a nonstandard way to allow for the zigzag graphic element created by placing all the cards in a row.

A Gardenia Greeting ►

Rows of gardenias mean that guests are greeted with a feast for the senses. The pungent scent of the flowers wafted invitingly toward guests even as they crossed the threshold of this event. Looking like an army troop marching off to duty, the gardenias were arranged individually in long rows, each in its own petite glass container. (Later in the evening, waiters pass out the gardenias as a farewell giveaway.) The place cards and their flower companions were arranged on a lustrous silver beaded and embroidered organza table covering. This effect gives guests a calming yet luxurious sense of order, rhythm, and decorum punctuated by the idea that what is to come will be rich, romantic, and dignified.

The Look of Tradition

What could be more welcoming than a large-scale topiary bursting with gorgeous blooms? More in the nature of a traditional escort-card table, this marble-topped console is elegant and simple enough to be the perfect spot for guests to pick up their assignations.

Hanging-Leaf Place Cards ▶

For this autumn event, leaves hanging in midair made the perfect place cards. Created from different colored papers and printed by graphic designer Matthew Sporzynski, this foliage was affixed to a box-shaped screen made of nearly transparent tulle. As guests entered the event they plucked their cards off the screen in a delightful twist on the traditional. The treelike topiary was decorated in glowing reds, yet its branches were semibare — a reminder of the season. The entire effect worked on the subtlest of levels, communicating the idea of autumn's falling leaves in an original and indirect way.

◄ A Country-Casual
Escort Arrangement

Most arrangements on escort tables are normally raised up away from the escort cards. Isn't it wonderful to see a floral design that seems to be spilling over toward the cards, threatening to engulf them? This draping of flowers makes the statement that abundance is the hallmark of what is to come. The guests had no choice but to take notice. To create a little tension for interest, we juxtaposed the formality of the surroundings with a wooden escort table. The arrangement is a bit out of control, while its large, belly-round terra-cotta pot is both country classic and suggestive of corpulent prosperity. There's a versatility to terra-cotta that can be played up or down as the case may be. Also, the casualness of the arrangement and the long rustic wooden table on which it was placed worked well together. The overall idea is to encourage guests to turn over control and place themselves in their hosts' hands for the evening.

Fluttering Place Cards
in an Outdoor Breeze ►

For this outdoor wedding, the client asked for something different. To create the escort arrangement, we built an arbor of flowers that matched the one we created for the ceremony. Each place card was pierced and bow tied with a pretty ribbon. Then we painstakingly tied the other end of each card to the frame of the arch. The dangling cards took on a celebratory air. Guests had only to approach the arbor and gently pull their card — a somewhat fanciful task, but one that added to the festive feeling of the event.

◄ Making Hallways Inviting

Here my client wisely asked me to be sure to create a decor for the corridors in the hotel in which her wedding was held. First we eliminated any distractions from the matter at hand, the party, by covering the existing walls with plain white cotton and making a scrim for the ceiling. We strung garlands of hydrangeas and red roses to hang along the entranceways and at the ceiling's edge. We avoided the glare of the ambient lighting by setting up simple spotlights. The passageways set the stage as festive, unencumbered entrées to the reception beckoning in the background.

An Entirely New Corridor Decor ►

At first glance this hallway may appear to be like any other leading to a ballroom. Look again. The elements that distinguish this hall have all been added. In keeping with the overall tone of her event, my client asked me to hide the existing architecture of the passageway. On closer inspection, you can see the screens we created out of translucent tulle. Even the ceiling and existing light fixtures were hidden by an archway of tulle. We installed new fixtures of electric pillar candles and bedecked them with blooms. Then, to create the dreamy play of light in the space, we uplighted the tulle screens from behind. The beams of light were diffused by the screens but still reached to the arched ceilings to create the reflection and light the tulle up above as well. Quite the elaborate effect for a passageway, but well worth it.

Consider also the actual entrance to the event. If your event is in your home, be sure to use your foyer as an area of decor. At a public venue such as a hotel, you may want to give the hallways leading to the room you are using some thought. Is there anything that can be done to impress your own style on them? Hinting in the corridors at what is to come is often a nice touch and one remembered by guests. For example, I have lined hallways with decorative screens that reflect the decor of the room ahead. I have also echoed the decor of an event in a corridor by creating floral arrangements to guide guests along their way. It is vital not to overlook the importance of the entrance to your party. As for tents, it is possible to create a vestibule in them that provides a transition space between the outdoors and the interior of the tent. In the previous chapter, for instance, we showed an entranceway in a tent that initiated the guests to the theme of the event. The Roman-style columns and arched doorway provided the bridge between the outside world and the fantasy world created within the tent.

Room dividers and screens

Most nonprofessionals are unaware of how useful barrier structures or partitions can be when working with different types of venues. The chief purpose of barriers is to divide a room and control flow. As discussed in the previous chapter, flow is the movement and grouping of your guests. If a room is too large, partitions will make it appear smaller and corral your guests into tighter, more intimate groupings. Barriers, of course, are also used to divide a room into functional areas. This might occur when you use a space for a dual purpose such as both cocktails and dinner or both the wedding ceremony and the reception. One use is to separate the entrance area from the space where the main event is held. Another is to create a separate, perhaps quieter sitting area. It's a common practice to set off the dance floor. Finally, barriers can serve as

Screens as a Backdrop for Couture

In keeping with his inventive style and love of the unusual, fashion designer John Galliano wanted a unique approach for presenting his latest collection. As we discussed his ideas, we began by questioning the main premise of all fashion shows: that models wearing the new designs walk out and parade them before the audience. Why not turn that idea on its head and have the clothing be static while the audience moves, not unlike viewing art in a museum or gallery? So Galliano decided to clothe mannequins in his collection, place them against a backdrop, then have the audience move around the room. This approach actually permits better viewing, since those in attendance can really look at the detailing and craftsmanship of the designs. The challenge was to create backdrops that not only complemented the fashions but also were of some interest in their own right. We also had to consider the venue, in this instance, New York's Metropolitan Club. The screens we created as the backdrops for the show were gilded in a manner similar to the old-world detailing in the room. This time we needed opacity, so we used white canvas printed with a light gold pattern. What made the screens interesting was that they were decorated with fresh flowers in very unusual patterns. As can be seen in the photo, however, the white canvas of the screens was the perfect frame for the clothing, while the floral decorations took nothing away from it.

camouflage for unsightly architectural details or fixtures that are an unavoidable aspect of rented venues.

Using screens is a very inventive and effective way to create a partition. I'm especially fond of them because you can play with them a bit. Frequently at events, potted plants or trees are rented to be used as barriers. In my opinion, this is a rather predictable approach. Moreover, trees don't function well as room dividers because the foliage is an uneven screen and only effective at a certain height. I prefer the use of screens or panels because they provide an enormous degree of latitude in enhancing the decor of the room.

You can have screens built out of wood or metal, then paint them to suit your decor. My favorite way to make a screen is to build a frame and tighten fabric over it, much like stretching a canvas. The fabric can be anything, opaque or translucent, depending on your aim. If you wish to create an area of privacy, use an opaque fabric. But if you want an interesting effect, use a fabric that is translucent. At one event, we set up a row of ten-foot screens using a gold translucent fabric and illuminated them to create a spectacular shimmering wall. A screen such as this is a perfectly functional barrier, yet because you can see through it, it generates a certain air of mystery in a room.

Another method that I use regularly is to digitally print images on the fabric I use for screens. This gives me tremendous leeway in terms of what I want to achieve, since any sort of decoration or image can be printed. At *Glamour* magazine's Woman of the Year awards, we printed the images of all the women being honored on the screens we erected. Often we'll uplight, backlight, or project onto a screen for even more effect.

Of course, a simple yet effective method is to just drape fabric to create a barrier. Draping or hanging fabric in a tent is a way to create functional areas and also add texture. At home the simplest thing in the world would be to hang a curtain or two to create a divider or to hide

Printed Imagery on Screens Enhances an Event's Purpose

At *Glamour* magazine's Woman of the Year awards, we were confronted with a large tent space that needed to be subdivided to create definite functional areas — entranceway, cocktail/bar area, dining, and dancing. The natural solution was to build a variety of screens. The question was, what kind of screens? In keeping with *Glamour*'s purpose of honoring women of achievement, we decided that photographs of all the honorees would go on the screens. We digitally printed the images on translucent fabric, then stretched this across a specially built frame. Created by digital imaging expert Michael Speir, all the images had a rose-petal border in red — symbolizing feminine power. The eight-by-ten-foot panels were the perfect solution for separating and defining the fifty-by-one-hundred-foot tent. The best thing about this type of process for creating a screen is the fact that you can print on see-through fabric. Then the right lighting, in this case uplighting, makes the images come alive. This type of screen is particularly wonderful because if it were opaque it would make for too-severe divisions in the room. This way, you manage to divide the space but gain a sense of openness and movement that is very effective visually.

Fanciful Wooden Partitions

This corporate event was held at an art gallery in lower Manhattan, where the client wanted to enable guests to see a particular exhibit. Galleries can be especially raw spaces and this one was no exception. This meant that we needed to find a way to separate the cocktail area, the entrance, and the dinner area. The Soho gallery featured modern art, in this case modern paintings in reds and blues that had a whimsical feel. Inspired by the artwork, we set about creating screens to match

the space. We had the idea of screens that were nearly sculptural — perhaps even Gaudi-esque — in aspect, though still two-dimensional. Cut out of plywood and painted in the same bright colors as the art, the screens were put together randomly and mirrored the artwork at the gallery in a way that was whimsical without being patronizing.

A Phosphorescent Wall of Gold

This venue is a monumental space in the Wall Street area of Manhattan. Its classical architecture with its Corinthian pillars is impressive, which does pose the problem of how to make the space more intimate. Tables should never be spread out to fill a space. Rather, keep tables together and surround guests with barriers to make them feel a bit cozier. In this case, we solved the problem by erecting a wall of ten-foot-high screens to surround the diners. We made the wall with one simple yet fantastic iridescent gold fabric and lit the screens to fabulous effect. Translucent screens such as these can be used to produce interesting impressionistic effects. In this case, we lit the candles on the tables, so as the guests walked in, they saw this wonderful vision of murky light flickering behind the golden gauzy screens. The screens' design created a wonderful illusion and was in perfect keeping with the integrity of the space, so it is easy to overlook how well the screens did their job: their golden color and the effect of lighting them added tremendous warmth to a space that might otherwise have felt cold; their height pierced the too-high ceilings and so improved the perception of dimension in the room; and finally, their use as a barrier to surround the guests created an intimacy that would otherwise have been missing.

some aspect of your home that you wish to remain unseen. Fabric is always a wonderful way to soften the hard edges of any venue. And drapery can be very cost-effective, since fabric bought in bulk can be quite inexpensive. In chapter 2 I showed how we created a scrim for the Meals on Wheels benefit that was particularly atmospheric, yet cost-effective as well.

Dance floors: often forgotten but always a focal point

It is traditional for dance floors to be set off in some way. Usually you see foliage or shrubbery placed around the dance floor. Often I will build a physical structure so the dance floor has its own canopy of floral decor. While this sets the physical boundaries of the dance floor, demarcating it and containing its energy, don't forget that the dance floor itself is a decor element. Though in ballrooms there is little reason to change the dance floor, some venues, particularly museums, don't usually have dance floors, so you'll have to build one. In addition, by necessity you might need to lay a floor when you erect a tent, and this includes the dance floor. Therein lies the opportunity for creativity.

Laying a wooden floor is expensive, though necessary and worth it. The beauty of wooden floors is that they can be painted and decorated to match your decor. It's a wonderful way to enhance the room and your vision. For example, the initials of the host and hostess can be painted in the center of the room. An anniversary party with a red theme can have a bright crimson-colored dance floor. Another method I have used for creating a highly unusual design for a dance floor is to digitally print the image of a pattern or other design onto huge portions of vinyl. These are then laid and fitted together to form the surface of the dance floor. It's a wonderful decor effect because the dance floor is such a focal point of a room.

A Hand-Painted Wooden Floor

This last image is that of a wooden dance floor laid in a tent. Though wooden flooring can be costly, you can see that it might be worth the extra expense. Not only is the surface easy to dance on, but if hand painted, as this one is, it can add a significant element to the decor of your event.

A Monumental Design in Vinyl

This dance floor was created for the event in the previous photo. Notice the wall of screens in the background. More obvious, however, is the large dance floor. This room's marble flooring is inappropriate for dancing. The way I solve this sort of situation is by laying vinyl flooring over the existing material. The wonderful thing about vinyl is that you can print on it. Thus you can create a floor in any sort of pattern or image that you might like. A dance floor is such a focal point, why not try something different with it? In this case, the monumental pattern we laid down was perfect for filling up the voluminous amount of space in the room.

A note on tableware and other details

Your choice of tableware for your place settings and the decor of the tables at your event is a deeply personal one. Be sure to take the time to investigate all your options. Whether you are using your own glassware, flatware, and china or will be renting them, these are items that deserve careful consideration. If the rental house doesn't have what you want, find one that does. And if you must use what's available at the location of your event, be sure to investigate your options. Then work to personalize your tables in some special ways. Much can be achieved with linens, flowers, and other extra items that you contribute yourself. Consider how you can add a special graphic or calligraphic touch to place cards or menus. Don't settle!

The above applies to the chairs you use as well. The classic ballroom chair is in evidence everywhere, but that doesn't mean you have no other choices. Other types of chairs are available if you are willing to look (and pay) for them. A simpler solution is to use a bit of creativity to dress up the seating. Organza and raw silk chair covers are becoming common today. Tie some ribbons to the back of seats for a bit of whimsy. Attach a floral bouquet to seat backs that guests are free to take home as a gift. Have specialty seat cushions made out of a favorite fabric, if you wish.

When executing your vision, the key ingredient of success is to look at each decision as an opportunity to do things in your own way. Refrain from accepting conditions as given. Let your sense of style prevail in every detail, and your guests are certain to notice.

Glass and Flowers As a Design Statement

Clear glass and orchids provided just the right design elements for the tables of this wedding reception. Notice how the careful choice of each detail makes the entire table come together. The tables' main floral arrangements were glass urns whose bases and lids were covered in miniature green mums and accented with cymbidium orchids. The tableware of green and golden tinted wineglasses on twisted stems and glass chargers perfectly mirrored the arrangements. In addition, monumental roses were "created" by placing individual petals in low glass bowls filled with water. Lower arrangements of pale green and yellow cymbidium orchids were placed at intervals atop the pistachio-colored raw silk tablecloths on the long tables. This fresh and soothing design calls to mind the aftereffects of a rain shower in early spring.

Chapter 6

LOWERS

HOW TO DESIGN THE PERFECT FLORAL DECOR

No event is complete without some kind of floral decor. You might design the perfect environment for your affair, but the flowers will be the crowning touch for personalizing your event. From time immemorial, celebrations have always been enhanced by flowers. Richly symbolic, flowers communicate so much just by being seen. The miracle of flowers — their beauty and delicacy in all their many varieties — is truly a gift from Mother Nature. Thus they are powerful statements of generosity of spirit. Symbolizing the life force as well, they imbue every event with the energy of their organic forms and the natural world. Nowhere are flowers more de rigueur than at weddings. This is because flowers have long been considered a symbol of love. In fact, around the turn of the eighteenth century and through the nineteenth, specific varieties of flowers would be given to express messages of love that the giver might have difficulty putting into words.

Flowers always generate a reaction. People respond, almost instinctively, not only to the natural beauty of flowers but also to the amazing and wonderful ways flowers enhance the ambience of an event. Above all else, let your flower arrangements make a statement appropriate to your event's overall design. If you want a lavish over-the-top affair, the arrangements must be that way too. If your aim is elegant simplicity, select flowers with clean lines and place them in dignified containers of the highest quality. Flower arrangements must always work in harmony with a party's theme. And because flowers are about generosity, don't even consider skimping on them. Flowers must be the greatest gift you give your guests.

The importance of your floral decor

When planning your event, choosing your floral decor will be one of your most important decisions. It is through flowers that you will truly articulate your vision, since flowers embody everything I've talked about thus far. Their color and texture set the mood; they can be used to transform a space and solve design problems; and because they are usually the focal point of both a room and a table, they will be one of the main ways for you to express yourself.

When choosing the flowers for your event, you don't have to follow any rules about flowers. You are completely free to select the varieties that you prefer. In fact, the ideal is for you to choose flowers that you are passionate about. Why not envelop your guests with what you love? Are you crazy for irises? Then use them. I had one client who adored wisteria, so we created a whole structure for nothing but wisteria blossoms. Think about the style or theme of your event, then evaluate all your floral options. Study flower and wedding books or even gardening magazines. Drop by your local florist to see what's in stock and to examine any catalogs available there. Choose flowers in colors that align with your vision for the mood of your event. Then reflect on their texture. How can the texture of the flowers you have chosen enhance the overall mood? Do you want sophisticated floral arrangements or something understated? Do you want a refined kind of flower or perhaps something that is wilder or more rustic?

Today most types of blooms are available year-round, so what you choose for your event has more to do with price than availability. Work

◄ Using Decorative Glass

For the event shown on page 112, we scoured antique shops for unique items to use as centerpieces, since we wanted a lavish, classical look. Among our finds was this gorgeous crystal urn with fantastic gold detailing. We raised it up and then surrounded it with every highly textured and richly colored flower imaginable, including roses, peonies, and orchids. We even strategically placed blooms on the urn itself, together with a few delicate red berries for some added charm. Using only warm-colored blossoms, oranges, reds, pinks, and burgundies, created a mood that was unusually luxurious. A gold embroidered organza table overlay and glass chargers whose gold edges almost appear to have been granulated by jewelry makers contribute even more warmth and opulence to the overall effect. Notice how the mono-chromatic color scheme on the table sets off and frames the textural richness of the centerpiece.

Vibrant Jewel Tones ►

This is a classic low centerpiece slightly oval in shape. These jewel-tone flowers make up one of my most requested color combinations. With black magic roses, hydrangeas, lilacs, poppies, and cattleya orchids, this arrangement can be described in one word: *vibrant*.

◀ A Textured Pastel Centerpiece

This photograph always elicits a great response from people. They seem to love this palette of springtime pastels in peach and green. The flowers, including lilacs, hydrangeas, miniature calla lilies, tulips, and roses, are wonderfully free and casual looking. On a subliminal level, people are undoubtedly responding to the amount of texture here. This is an extremely sensuous bouquet. All the flowers in this arrangement, right down to the parrot tulips, have a great deal of dimension. The table linens also create texture. One of our signature effects is to put a flower in each napkin, in this case a cattleya orchid. It's a type of repetition. Here the cloth of the napkin is arranged to mirror the form of the orchid, which only contributes more texture to the scene. The cattleya orchid is the archetypal glamorous orchid flower owing to its soft feminine ruffles and the delicacy of its petals — again, a flower with texture.

A Two-Tiered Centerpiece ▶ with a Twist

This is an example of a two-tiered centerpiece. The bottom tier is a profusion of sumptuous hot-colored flowers in reds, oranges, and pinks that nearly fills the center of the table. The top tier is a fairly traditional candelabra with pillars and more lush blooms. Yet it sits on a very unusual stand made of twisted and burnished metal, organic in form and evoking movement. Because the stand is artistic and contemporary, it becomes a point of interest, yet it still provides for clear sight lines. A two-tiered effect such as this is a feast for the eyes, since it provides not only a variety of focal points to entertain guests but also an amazing abundance of color and texture.

with a floral designer or florist to find out what will be in season or can be obtained easily at the time of your event if you want to know what will be more cost-effective. Domestic peonies are available only in early summer, for example. And you'd be hard-pressed to find dogwood or cherry blossoms in the fall. Of course, if you can't live without them, certain out-of-season flowers are available from other regions in the world, such as the southern hemisphere, but importing them may put a dent in your budget. Luckily, there are many flowers that are readily available year-round, such as all those wonderful types of roses and orchids.

Arrangements

While there is little room for improvement upon a flower, we have long known how exciting it is to bring flowers together in masses. There's a tremendous pleasure in grouping flowers of the same variety into bunches, but there is also a thrill to mixing differing varieties and colors.

Any flower arrangement automatically becomes a focal point. It draws people's attention and so becomes a statement in its own right. The three types that are generally on view at most events are center-pieces, larger-scale or monumental arrangements, and topiaries. Every arrangement — whether it is a small posy-type grouping of roses in a low vase or a ten-foot floral sculpture — should be dramatic. You have to make it exciting. Why go to all the trouble to assemble flowers only for the end result to be ordinary? However, arrangements that are too contrived don't work either. For example, I dislike the use of props (other than those that are natural, such as tree branches or fruit) in floral arrangements. Props make the floral decor look a bit too cutesy for my taste. One of the most arduous tasks for any person doing a party or designing flowers is to walk the fine line between trying too hard and boredom.

Filling Out Space with Large-Scale Metal Vessels

Containers come in every possible material and shape today, but I still find that there are occasions when it's best to create your own. Here I was confronted with the problem that the space for this business event was larger than what was really needed. This gathering was for a small select group of the firm's clients, but the venue could have been used for many more people. We felt that we needed to fill out the room, so we decided to do something very sculptural and created these metallic cone-shaped containers, which we filled with tall spring-blossoming branches, spirea and viburnum. The metal containers created substance and solidity, while the unusual shape fit in nicely with this contemporary art gallery. For that modern look, everything was in muted tones of white. The effect was a success. Even though there weren't a lot of tables, when you walked through the space, you felt as though the room were full.

In my opinion, floral arrangements should copy nature as closely as possible. There is tremendous opportunity for creativity, however, because you are not confined by what is possible in nature. Copy what you see in nature, such as the repetition of color and texture, movement in the form of spilling over or drooping, and balancing other colors with green. In this last case, the green doesn't necessarily have to mean greenery. Shift things around a bit and use flowers or other botanicals that come in hues of green, such as pale green hydrangeas, celadon chrysanthemums, sage-colored amaranthus, or even verdigris berries. The result is a pleasing surprise that still reflects nature's glory.

Repetition is one of your best tools. Like rhythm in a musical composition, repeating certain themes throughout your various arrangements will produce an energy or vitality in the room. You can achieve repetition in a number of ways. One is by making sure that a selected variety is repeated or used the same way over and over again. Another is by repeating the shape or size of an arrangement. One of my favorite effects is to use a flower in a simple way but repeat it throughout a room. For example, you could place a single orchid in its own plain wooden box, then multiply this by a hundred and put them all over a room. This effect, while simple, produces a very exciting result. Presenting just one type of flower en masse creates a very clean, contemporary, and vibrant effect.

To continue the musical metaphor a bit, you also want to create a melody or main floral theme to run throughout your event. Perhaps this is a color or a scheme of colors, or a specific variety of blooms. This will be what best expresses the overall mood or theme. Finally, create harmony with other types of flowers by adding contrast in the form of texture, if you've chosen a monochromatic color scheme, or in the form of different colors or even entirely different species of botanicals, such as fruits, berries, plants, or foliage. Trust your instincts as to what works in a harmonious way. If something doesn't feel quite right, try something else.

A Sculptural Terra-Cotta Container

A wonderfully interesting terra-cotta container was the basis for this unusual centerpiece. It set the stage for the overall earthiness of the arrangement. Emerging from its sculptural base are two *putti*-like figures valiantly sustaining the large shallow vessel above. The flowers seem to explode in a welter of hot autumnal tones. Amaranthus and pepper berries dripping from the container's edge make the centerpiece feel a little more rustic or natural and perfectly evoke nature's wild beauty.

When planning your arrangements, remember to consider scale. First, arrangements should always be in proportion to the scale of the room. A large space with an enormous vault of a ceiling will demand large-scale floral designs, while a small, intimate dinner would seem ridiculous with a too-large centerpiece soaring to the ceiling and looming over the guests. Second, the size of the flowers used should also be in proportion to the size of the arrangement. Large blossoms look overblown and silly in a small nosegay. Meanwhile, small garden roses and buds will be drowned out and barely visible in oversize arrangements, topiaries, or ceiling effects.

Centerpieces

Everyone has heard the rule of thumb that centerpieces should not rise so high as to obscure the vision or conversation of guests who sit across from one another at a table. Though this makes good sense, this directive needn't limit your creativity in any way. I frequently solve the problem by raising arrangements *up* above eye level. Then, because you also want guests to have something lovely to look at, I often create a smaller low arrangement at the base of the higher one. This two-tiered approach is very effective, particularly when you want to add some height or drama to a room. If cost is a consideration, you could put two-tiered arrangements on every other table and a lower version on the alternates. Another reason for this approach is that if certain centerpieces are more like topiaries, it's best to alternate them simply because they can be overwhelming. One item I don't put in the prop category is candelabras. A truly lovely raised centerpiece is often a candelabra holding strikingly tall taper candles and positively dripping with flowers.

The containers or holders you choose for your centerpieces should reflect both your taste and the event's theme. The variety of containers is limitless. Be artful. Dream up different and unique ways to hold

Sculptural Metallic Containers at the Museum of Modern Art

We took an approach here similar to the previous image by creating metallic containers for this event on the patio of the sculpture garden at the Museum of Modern Art. We wanted to create something modern, sculptural, organic, and large scale to fit into the environment of the garden. So we approached a metal sculptor to produce the containers and weld the stands to them. For an additional effect, the metal was distressed. The flowers were kept simple; the main blooms were Casablanca lilies and hydrangeas — both big flowers for these big containers. We even filled similar containers that were somewhat shorter and placed them on the sidewalk outside the museum to welcome arriving guests.

Classic Topiary Shapes
with Sugared Grapes

As can be seen when viewing the room as a whole, these centerpieces created an impressive scale at this wedding reception. Some were nearly six feet high! But their height dressed up the room. The main part of the centerpiece was a great globe of flowers in creams, pinks, and burgundies set on a tree branch firmly rooted in a terracotta pot. Both the pot and the branch were gold leafed. Various-colored roses, hydrangeas, dahlias, and even snapdragons were mixed with some flat eucalyptus berries. Gently curving down the branch is a garland of blooms laden with grapes, which rests, finally, on the table. Part of

what makes this centerpiece so appealing is the different grapes hanging from the garland. Groupings of bunches were also placed as additional centerpieces at intervals on the bride and groom's central rectangular table. Sugar-coated grapes are easily created by dipping the bunches in confectioner's sugar. The ambient lighting in this room at New York's Metropolitan Club can be dimmed, which was the preference of the host and hostess. Although dim lighting is atmospheric, in such light it is important to spotlight arrangements with at least three spots, as shown here.

Metal Hearts and Flowers

For this Valentine's Day party at the Puck Building in New York, we wanted center-pieces with some height. So we had a sculptor solder together these fanciful metal hearts, each one slightly different from the others. Some hearts were thinner, some heavier, some taller. We mounted them on stands and entwined them with smilax. We clustered roses at the foot of the hearts as a small focal point for the tables and adorned the hearts with them as well. For variety, we alternated red and white roses at the tables. Clustering flowers of the same color together can make quite an impact.

arrangements in place. Traditional terra-cotta containers come in any number of shapes and sizes. Moreover, they can be painted or gilded in any way you can imagine. Glass or crystal is often classically elegant. But certainly, flower stems don't need to show, so fill glass vases with anything of interest: pinecones, berries, fruit, petals, pebbles, or additional flowers themselves. Silver urns and vases always denote elegance. At home, consider using glass and porcelain serving bowls, fancy cake plates, compotes, or family silver. One way to keep arrangements looking interesting and to create some tension is to vary the containers you use. For example, choose a variety of cut crystal in different shapes and heights. Or you could be even more personal by using family heirlooms or a collection of some kind — your collection of cobalt blue Depression glass or McCoy pottery, for example. It is often my practice to design and construct the holders for my clients. We can thus truly give imagination a free rein.

Large-scale arrangements

Large-scale arrangements are appropriate in a number of cases. Sometimes you want to place a monumental arrangement at the center of a room to act as an anchor and to provide a focal point. Often larger-scale arrangements are strategically placed to attract guests' attention away from any flaws in the room. And as seen earlier, the height of arrangements can do much to pierce spaces that are cavernous.

Target areas that your guests will frequent for large-scale arrangements. Because they are dramatic and glamorous, larger arrangements should be used in areas where people spend the most time, such as the entranceway, escort table, buffets, or other stations. In these locations, people are more apt to see them and be struck by them. Larger-scale arrangements provide a great opportunity to create a visual impact. For these arrangements you want to use anything that gives height. Set them on tables to raise them up. Lift them farther by placing them on

A Cascading Waterfall of Blooms

When we designed this multitiered arrangement, we wanted to call to mind the motion of water — to create a veritable waterfall of flowers. First we set up glass containers at various heights. Then we filled them with an overflow of blooms, which we allowed to hang loosely over their edges together with dripping berries and amaranthus. The minute flowers of the amaranthus are borne in drooping tassel-like spikes, making this type of perennial a favorite for any flower arrangement involving hanging effects. To re-create this design you need to have several different shapes of glass containers, some to be used as pedestals for the others. Rather than leave the containers empty, be creative and playful with the transparency of the glass. Fill them with fruit, berries, or flowers, as shown here. This arrangement was the perfect companion to the mouth-watering offerings of a dessert buffet.

Magical cherry blossoms towering above an assortment of seafood is a classic buffet image. This corporate event at the Guggenheim Museum was a cocktail party in conjunction with a special exhibit. The museum is a very open space, noted for its unusual design (based around a continuous spiral ramp like the inside of a seashell), which allows guests to wander from one floor to another. On each floor a few buffet stations were set up. To reflect the architecture of the museum itself, cleanness and openness were the hallmarks of the occasion, including the presentation for the buffets. Since all buffet arrangements require some substance and height, the obvious choice was the unsullied beauty of simple cherry blossoms.

other containers or raised platforms. Use natural elements and flowers that have height as well. Tree branches such as cherry blossoms, dogwood, or birch are good. Remember that flowers should be large, solid blooms such as peonies, hydrangeas, dahlias, zinnias, and chrysanthemums. Though lilies are often used in such designs, I have to say I find them to be ordinary.

Buffets are where you can really put your most dramatic arrangements. Buffet tables are important. All guests visit them at one point or another. You don't want to interfere with the table's function by overemphasizing the decoration, yet you want to do something truly unique. Be sure to consider and incorporate whatever else will be at the buffet station. Sometimes this requires a bit of planning, and you might want to call the caterer or the hotel to find out what kind of containers they're using and what will be served where — make it a joint venture. Then you can plan to put on a wonderful display. There are a few secrets to it. First, repetition is important, and second, there should be a generosity about it. If you're displaying bread, make sure the selection is huge and plentiful. If it's a floral arrangement, make sure you repeat the color of the flower or the same flower as often as possible. Clustering flowers enables you to create blocks of color in the arrangement.

Topiaries are large-scale standing arrangements that are sculptural in nature. They consist of a form covered with flowers and can really be any shape. Topiaries are useful as barriers, but I usually use them along the aisles or at the altar of a wedding ceremony, or to flank entranceways or bandstands. Wedding ceremonies require some sort of large-scale adornment and people often use trees or topiaries. A common topiary shape simulates the look of a tree by creating a globe of blooms set on a wooden stem from a tree branch. This is then placed in a pot or container as a base. Garlands might also adorn the stem. Another topiary shape is an arch used as a backdrop or canopy for the altar at a wedding ceremony. A favorite of mine is a shape that looks like a large spiral of blooms.

◄ An Overflow of Abundance

Abondanza! It's a volcanic eruption of nature's bounty. This mini–Mount Vesuvius was created by building a monumental frame that we adorned with a plethora of roses, dahlias, hydrangeas, and grapes of every variety. The spirit of this arrangement is so generous that it envelops even the breads and other items being offered at this buffet table. Here we worked with the caterer to produce a jointly designed buffet. And one can hardly miss its location either!

Peacock Topiary ►

This peacock topiary was created as the buffet arrangement at the Indian-theme luncheon given by Joan Rivers that I discussed in chapter 1. Inventive and out of the ordinary, it was one of many unusual decor effects that Joan asked us to create. A peacock was the perfect shape to imitate for many reasons. Not only did it originate in India, but it is also considered to be the bird of royalty. In many cultures it is considered to be a symbol of the sun. In addition, the large array of its fan means it's perfect for a larger-scale arrangement. We started by creating the topiary frame out of chicken wire. The fun part was finding the flowers, textures, and other elements to replicate the fan and other aspects of the peacock. We used ferns, hypericum, leucospermum, dendranthema, delphinium, orchids, and roses. The final result was hugely successful, since we placed peacock topiaries on all the consoles in the room. When guests arrived, they were immediately struck by a flock of wonderful, colorful peacocks.

The Tree of Life

A favorite design of mine is one I named the Tree of Life. In order to symbolize growth and spirit, we came up with the idea to create an effect designed to look like a tree. We begin with real tree branches planted in a base or a container of some kind. Then we affix different types of flowers, fruits, or berries to it to mimic leaves and tree blossoms. It's very organic. Make sure the branches you choose have a beautiful shape. You can create quite a lot of different textures and shapes by how you arrange the flowers on the tree. The wonderful thing about these "trees" is that they can vary from starkly beautiful to highly textured and full. Adapt your design to your vision for your event. The Tree of Life works beautifully as a large-scale design, since it

has height. It brings an outdoor element inside. You can have a lot of fun simply deciding how you are going to decorate yours. Also, it is somewhat unexpected or unusual, which adds interest.

I use a monochromatic color scheme in each of the three images shown here of a Tree of Life. The first two trees shown were used on buffet tables, while the last tree stood on the floor and served as an entrance arrangement. The first tree is decorated with cream-colored roses and cymbidium orchids, together with flat eucalyptus berries, green grapes, and verdant hydrangeas. It is the most highly textured of the three — as though the tree were in the full bloom of springtime. For the violet tree — the one you could imagine seeing

in the depths of summer — we used two different types of flowers, lavender-colored roses and hydrangeas, for an interesting textured result. The red tree is covered in roses, clustered together almost in the shape of pom-poms or balls, as though the tree were laden with a harvest of autumnal fruit.

I also like the fact that trees have wonderfully life-affirming symbolic and spiritual meanings in various religions and mythologies: to name a few, they can be found in Scandinavian mythology as the world tree Yggdrasil, in Genesis in the Bible as the tree of knowledge, and in Buddhism as the bodhi tree, under which the Buddha gained enlightenment.

Traditional Wedding Pastels
for a Ceremony at Home

For this wedding ceremony at home, we completely transformed the main living area of my client's house with flowers. All the floral effects were in classic pastels of apricots, peaches, pinks, and, of course, wedding creams. Large-scale arrangements require an appropriate scale in flowers and to this end, in conjunction with multicolored roses and dahlias, we used pale green hydrangeas. The high windows along one wall were the perfect backdrop for the altar. To frame the wedding couple and officiant, we created a huge floral arch that stood on the low windowsill. Then we festooned the existing drapes with more blooms for good measure. The two-story height of the room permitted twelve-foot topiary arrangements in a classic shape. We took advantage of the existing columns by draping them with more garlands, which faintly mimicked those on the arrangements. We even flooded the mantelpiece with our chosen array of blooms.

Wedding Whites in Spiraling Forms

The wonderful spiraling forms of this floral decor add considerable energy to the aisle of this wedding ceremony held at the St. Regis Hotel. A favorite wedding decor of many brides, the classic ivories, creams, and whites in these arrangements were punctuated with green in the form of hydrangea leaves and fit this classical room in gold and white perfectly. My clients requested that the wedding canopy be especially lush with flowers, so each of the supports was fully laden with blooms. We even created two large-scale spiraling topiaries for either side of the chuppah. The result was a classic wedding decor.

A Gilt Signature:
A Living Still Life

Many years ago I worked at Christie's, an international auction house, and the composition and look of the paintings there influenced my design vision. As I studied the wonderfully framed floral still lifes by the masters, I found myself attracted to their magnificent composition and scale. And I often wondered if there was a way of simulating those images with actual flowers. The image in my mind was akin to a still life, only fresh flowers were bursting forth from it. The two-dimensional became three-dimensional, with depth and texture as well as the vibrancy of real flowers.

Long afterward I actually went to Christie's and bought some of those fantastic large-proportioned antique gilded frames. Then I experimented in order to find a way to create a trompe l'oeil of any vase. I discovered that with digital printing you can take a photograph of anything, enlarge it to the size needed, and print it on canvas or any other fabric, which can then be stretched across the picture frame. Then, working with wire and florist's oasis, you can build any design you'd like in conjunction with the image on the canvas. These "living still lifes" are a signature of mine.

I've used these frames and this process in many, many ways: as the backdrop for an event, to decorate a traditional room, to hide existing detailing, as screens and room dividers, or just to hang on the wall as additional decor. I love them because they've solved many a design problem for me. Other people love them because they're unusual and a bit of a surprise.

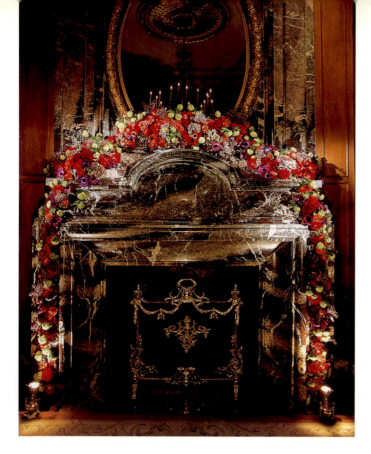

Decorating a Mantelpiece

The wonder of what can be achieved with flowers can be seen in the effects created by two different approaches to the fireplace at the St. Regis Hotel. In the first photo we festooned the slate-colored marble mantelpiece of the fireplace with a lush variety of flowers in reds and purples. All different colors and textures are represented. In the second, we draped it with a single type of orchid in one breathtakingly gorgeous color of pink and added a few well-placed pillar candles, making for a softly romantic effect.

A Monumental Floral Candelabra ▶

There are two beautiful existing chandeliers in the Plaza Hotel's Grand Ballroom, but we wanted to create something floral that would fit the dimensions of the room. Having studied the basic shape of a specific candelabra at a museum in France, we built one to scale with the help of a welder. Holding nearly a hundred electric pillar candles, each almost a yard in height, the whole structure was covered in thousands of fresh flowers. Hanging from the center of the ballroom's ceiling, it was a unique focal point for the evening, one that tied together the theme of all the floral arrangements below. Guests summed it up in two words: *monumental* and *unforgettable*.

Using Flowers As Gifts

Often a host or hostess of an event will give a small gift to guests. Some of my clients give flowers as a gift, while others will use flowers to enhance a gift. In the first image shown small bouquets are placed in wire gift baskets. Not only are the nosegays a token of appreciation, but the baskets can be used as handy storage containers later. One hostess gave the gift of flowers in the form of bulbs. Bulbs represent not only life but the promise of springtime. Flowers can be wonderfully versatile. With a little ingenuity, they can be used to decorate gift boxes for a gorgeous and unusual effect. Here the white orchids, which grace an ecru-colored wooden box, only hint at what goodies must lie within. Remember that removable lids are best, otherwise your guests won't open their presents for fear of disturbing the lovely miniature arrangements on top.

Other uses of flowers

Flowers can enhance your party in a myriad of surprising and playfully unexpected ways. They truly represent nature's bounty because what you can do with them is seemingly limitless. As some of the images presented in this book show, you can create wreaths, garlands, wall ornaments, trellises, even hanging structures for ceilings with flowers. If you wish, you can create gift boxes wrapped in blooms by gently affixing fresh buds or petals with a glue gun. A favorite practice of mine is to place a single exquisite bloom, often an orchid or rose, at every place setting, usually with the napkin. When guests arrive to sit down, they know that this is a gift just for them — a kiss from the universe. Chair backs can also be adorned with small arrangements of perfect blossoms. Outdoors, you may wish to craft a floral arch or trellis to guide guests to where you want them to go. Working with flowers to concoct your floral arrangements can be one of the most enjoyable and creative aspects of planning your event. Enjoy!

A Wisteria Canopy

A client with a deep passion for wisteria blossoms was anxious to use these blooms at her event. Wisteria is actually a vine, but the wisteria flower grows in drooping clusters one to one and one-half feet long. Wisteria blooms for only a short time and gives a beautiful scent. To best display the flowers in a way that is most natural to the plant, we decided to build an arborlike structure across the ceiling of this room at the St. Regis Hotel and to hang the violet-colored wisteria flowers from it. My client was overjoyed because she entertained under a virtual canopy of sweet-smelling wisteria all evening.

Chapter 7

BRINGING IT ALL TOGETHER

DEDICATION TO A VISION

Planning and orchestrating a successful event can require the coordination of countless details and, not infrequently, the management of any number of talented individuals engaged to help you fulfill your vision. How does one person manage to stay on top of the myriad decisions that must be made while also succeeding in stamping an event with his or her own personal style? Focus. It has been my experience that the hosts and hostesses of the most successful events not only take the time to articulate a meaningful concept for their event but keep this vision at the forefront as they make all the many decisions that they later encounter. Not only that, they make it their business to be sure that no decision is made without them. They don't ever take the path of least resistance; instead they question the process every step of the way to ensure that things are done in a manner that will maximize not only their own comfort level but that of their guests as well. The ability to concentrate on your desired goals throughout the design process is what takes the energy of an event up that extra notch to distinguish it as a truly extraordinary happening.

Any event will have its challenges. Often the biggest challenge will be to keep your focus as you bring your ideas to a particular venue. It is important to be able to adapt your vision to a room or location without losing it. When encountering obstacles, do not neglect your vision! At such a time it becomes more important than ever to stick to your guns. A solution to any problem is always found and usually it is in keeping with your desired goals — provided you don't let go of them. In addition, as with any endeavor, it is in overcoming challenges that the most interesting designs and effects are created.

Earlier chapters showed you how to organize your thoughts about your event. They gave you some ideas of what to consider when planning it and encouraged you to be as open-minded and creative as possible in order to make your event truly your own. Throughout this book, I have demonstrated my ideas about event decor and how important it is to create a "total decor concept" with photographs of many of the events that I have been privileged to be a part of. But these snapshots of a moment in time often can't fully represent what happens when everything comes together with a kind of magical flow, making for that perfect, memorable occasion that people talk about for weeks, if not years.

Hoping to convey some of that magic, in this chapter I present five separate events in more depth. Each of these events is a real statement, which is attributable to the vision, dedication, and focus of the person giving the party. Each is distinctive in its own way and each was a complete success. What do I mean by success? In terms of decor, the client and I created a complete concept for the event, planning each detail with the utmost consideration, resulting in a wholly unique and memory-filled experience for all who attended it. This doesn't mean to say that these events did not present challenges — all events do. In fact, part of the reason I include them here is precisely because each one illustrates a situation that is a bit out of the ordinary, for which we generated some interesting solutions.

The first two events were for Oprah Winfrey. When Oprah launched her highly successful magazine *O*, she wanted to give it the right send-off. As you might guess, for a woman of Oprah's stature, the right send-off meant inviting a thousand people to a reception and performance by

Tina Turner! Accommodating that number of people was quite an interesting proposition, but with some forethought and planning, everything went off without a hitch.

The following year, Oprah asked me to help her with another celebration, this time to mark the magazine's successful first year. Given that the launch party was widely considered to be a huge success, one very much remarked upon and written about in the press, it was a hard act to follow. Oprah wanted to work with the same decorating themes as in the first event but with a different underlying concept. Therein lay the challenge of the second event for O.

The third event in this chapter is a wedding. The hostess wanted to hold both the ceremony and the reception in the same space, the Grand Ballroom at the Pierre Hotel, but she wanted the decor of each to be so totally different that you'd hardly know you were in the same room. As you can imagine, this was quite a design challenge. How do you so completely transform a room from one type of event to another that it is unrecognizable in the space of an hour? For this kind of magic, we needed a bit of wizardry.

While each of the events presented in this volume is unique, the other wedding in this chapter is particularly special. This is due in large part to the attention to every detail lavished on the event by its hostess. This is a truly amazing story of what you can do with focus and dedication to an idea. Part of the idea, however, was a specific floral look or bloom that just wasn't in season. The challenge for me was in helping my client create the same look but with the flowers that were available at that time of year.

Finally, I present one of my favorite events. You encountered this event in chapter 1. It's the "pink-and-blue" party. As you might recall, the host and hostess of this event have a special passion for decorating in pink and blue. I love how they stick to their vision and won't compromise it, even in the least detail. I was asked to help the hosts transform a tent to be nothing less than an extension of their French provincial–style country house — to literally re-create the look of their home in another setting. This hostess's expression of her own unique style was an inspiration both to me and to her guests.

What these events all have in common is how aptly they illustrate the fantastic results that can be achieved by envisioning a concept and then insisting on finding a way to actualize it. Each of the clients in this chapter had a clear vision of what was wanted and was adamant about adhering to that vision, without compromise. While I helped them develop and execute their goals, these clients clearly knew what they wanted. More than that, they succeeded in remaining focused on their vision through all phases of the process, from the gathering of ideas to the practicalities of making the event happen. As you will see, the energy and effort that went into going that extra mile were well worth it. And I encourage you to do the same, whatever your event. Not only will you love the result, your guests will never forget it.

THE *O* LAUNCH
PARTY FOR OPRAH

New York is the publishing capital of the United States and home to Oprah Winfrey's new magazine, *O*. She and her staff came to me to ask for my help with the decor of the magazine's launch party. Oprah wanted to create a party that was vibrant, exciting, and dramatic, one with very contemporary or clean design lines — in other words, she wanted to reflect the design of the new magazine itself. It was to be a hot New York party, a cutting-edge soiree for a thousand people. It is impossible to seat so many people, so the food was served buffet style and the majority of the guests stood. Though the food was plentiful, in some ways it was more akin to a cocktail party. Later it became a concert as Tina Turner gave a rollicking performance.

Oprah and her staff had a very clear concept of what they wanted and kept that focus throughout our working together. Our first task was to find a clean, open space, one that was more modern in its look but that could also accommodate the expected number of guests. The Metropolitan Pavilion was chosen because it is a large, primarily white space with the look of a downtown art gallery. The beauty of it is that it is like a blank canvas, one that permits any variety of effects. If you want to create drama in a clean space such as this, use repetition. The more you repeat the same themes, the more dramatic it looks.

The sheer scale of the party, a thousand people, was an amazing logistical challenge. Any decoration might be lost in the shuffle of so many people. We realized that the ceiling was the one area where we could make an encompassing statement. In designing a space, there are three areas of a room to consider. To picture this, dissect the space in your mind's eye into three horizontal sections like a cake. Then decide how you will work with the ceiling, the middle section, and the lower part of the room. In the case of the *O* party, the lower part of the room would mainly be filled with guests. That meant that if we were going to create something visually exciting in a room full of people, it had to be at the ceiling, where it could be seen above everyone's heads.

The Decor

In meeting with Oprah, considering different ideas, and discussing various ways to approach the room, we decided to fill the entire ceiling with pink cherry blossoms. What better way to signify a new beginning than the quintessential bloom of spring? In order to achieve this effect, we had large sculptural containers custom made out of Plexiglas to hold the massive groupings

of cherry blossom branches and then hung them from the ceiling. The translucent white containers worked well in the room and were especially dramatic because they were also lit from within, suggesting lanterns, so that they emitted a moonlike glow. The repetition of the containers throughout the space created a wonderful vision of color, light, and texture.

The entrance to any event is incredibly important. It sets the tone and the mood for the entire event. This event was no exception. As we puzzled over ideas for the entranceway, it came to me to use the wonderful graphic O that had been designed as the logo for the magazine. So we re-created that O out of thousands of red flowers and then guests walked through the O as they entered the event. It was the perfect statement for the entrance. The symbol was repeated elsewhere at the event as well.

At an event of this size, any floral decor must be of a certain scale as well. Sometimes people rent trees to fill in a room, but we wanted to do something more imaginative. Inspired by the spiritual quality of the weeping willow tree, we mimicked it by creating four twelve-foot-high trees made entirely with cymbidium orchids, some pink, some yellow, and some green. The trees were suggestive of Asian design and were the perfect large-scale floral decor for a room of clean lines.

Lighting

For any room filled with people, it's best to make sure the perimeters of the room are well lit to open up the space and add depth. In addition, for this event we uplighted the columns for drama. If a room has any columns, it's always a good idea to light them. At night the eye tends to lose detail, so highlighting the columns immediately gives the room proportion. Naturally, we also spotlighted the containers of cherry blossoms as well as the buffets.

Buffets

Buffets and bars were set up around the room with food and beverages so that the guests could help themselves. Oprah's generosity of spirit, evident everywhere, was particularly apparent in terms of the abundance of wonderful food offered. We wanted the floral decor at the buffets to match this exuberance, and because they would be so visible, we wanted them to be perfect. For drama, energy, and warmth, the colors at the stations were all hot. We used magenta, fuchsia, apricot, and hot peach for the floral arrangements and also in the raw silk table and buffet overlays. These colors created a wonderful dynamism. In fact, they mirrored the colors used in the design of the new magazine. For several of the buffets, we filled a number of clear glass containers to overflowing with blooms, and by grouping them together, made them appear to be one massively abundant arrangement. Other floral effects for the buffets were trays of flower petals delicately positioned in wooden boxes. Repeated around the room, they were an enchanting design detail for anyone who encountered them.

One secret to any event is that if you want to move people, put food and drink wherever you want them to go. So we set up buffets by the concert stage in order to encourage the guests to be in place when Tina was ready to perform. To decorate the stage and its environs, we created screens printed with another form of the magazine's logo, this one shot on a background of gorgeous red petals. The party was topped off when Tina performed in front of these giant O's to a crowd wild with enthusiasm and good cheer.

THE ONE-YEAR ANNIVERSARY CELEBRATION FOR *O*

A year after the launch of *O,* Oprah gave an anniversary party to celebrate the magazine's very successful first year. The challenge in this case was that despite, or perhaps because of, the huge success of the first event, it was important that this second party look totally different while at the same time play with some of the same elements. Moreover, we were again faced with a guest list of roughly a thousand people. As for a theme, whereas the launch party was about new beginnings, the first-anniversary party was much more about celebration, the happy success of a venture, stability, and the notion that the magazine was here to stay. Otherwise the event was similar in that it was a reception with buffets for food and cocktails, followed by a performance. This time the idea was for the event to be more a dance party than a concert. The lucky guests were entertained by the O'Jays, one of Oprah's favorite groups.

The Venue

For a totally different look, Cipriani 42nd Street was chosen as the location for the anniversary party. This is a powerful venue that makes quite a statement. It is all about solid tradition and classical decor. In fact, the building itself was originally a bank. What better location to celebrate a successful venture! The scale of the room is also appropriate for an event of this size. Lined with monumental columns supporting broad arches, it is known for its fabulously high ceiling.

The Decor

Given not just the scale of the party but the power of the room itself, any decor for this event needed to be grand enough not only to be noticed but also to make a real statement. Though we used the hot, jazzy, energetic colors that are really a trademark of the magazine's design, just as we had for the launch party, we also went more into a deeper palette of jewel tones. We chose rubies, emeralds, sapphire-purples, and crystal whites, since they betoken good fortune and opulence.

Similar to the first party, the number of people at this party necessitated that the decor make a bold statement at the ceiling. This was even more important given its height. High ceilings always give guests a feeling of wonderful freedom and that sense of loftiness and breathing room, yet they require attention as well. Because the space is so classical, we created giant flower-bedecked chandeliers with electric pillars to hang in the upper part of the room. They created an immediate impact on whoever entered. Though they look as though they are covered in feathers, in actuality the French-style chandeliers were decorated with hand-dyed magnolia leaves together with masses of roses. Festive, decorative, and playful, they look as though they belong at the Moulin Rouge.

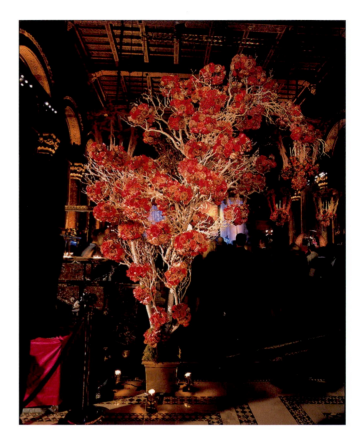

Trees of Life

The entrance was flanked by two twenty-foot-tall Trees of Life to symbolize the growth of the magazine over the last year. These "trees" were ripe with red roses, a powerful and dynamic color. Elsewhere, other smaller-size trees graced the buffets, each with a different color scheme.

The *O* Logo

To highlight the logo of the magazine once more, we again worked with it to create eight-foot-tall O's, which were placed just before the entrance to the dance floor. These O's were made of the same hand-dyed magnolia leaves in shades of deep reddish burgundy as were used to decorate the chandeliers. Within each O we placed tall cascading flower arrangements pouring from stamped silver containers. Vaguely reminiscent of fountains, the arrangements — made with orchids, roses, lilacs, and hydrangeas — brought to mind the generosity and abundance of ceaselessly flowing water.

The Stage and Dance Floor

Since this was a dance party, the stage and dance floor were especially dramatic. Digital printing expert Michael Speir created a dance floor covered with the same O logo as was used on the party's invitations by laying down panels of vinyl printed with it. The stage, built for the event, was draped with hundreds of yards of fabric. Then we produced a twenty-foot image of the cover of the magazine as the backdrop for the stage. That month's cover theme, joy, was a happy accident that serendipitously proved to be the perfect expression for the energy and infectious mood of a wonderful evening.

TRANSFORMING A ROOM FROM A CEREMONY TO A RECEPTION

The next two events, both weddings, stand out because in each case the client hosting the event knew her own taste and exactly what she wanted to achieve. In the case of this event, the hostess is a woman who thinks big and is undaunted by obstacles, timetables, or other challenges. And why not? After all, this was her wedding, and she was perfectly entitled to ask that her dreams become a reality. That's what weddings are all about. However, she presented me with an interesting problem: in the space of an hour we needed to completely transform a room from one decor to another. The wedding was to be held in the Grand Ballroom at the Pierre Hotel, and the idea was to use it for both the ceremony and the reception—but to make the decor of each totally different. And for both, the mood was to be lavish and magical, a fairy-tale setting for a fairy-tale wedding. In addition, my client has a particular depth of feeling for flowers. It is her belief that they should really be a presence at an event. So, she wanted not only to fill her event with them but also to use them in every possible and unusual way—even on the ceiling! Clearly this is a woman who likes to make a statement.

The Decor

My first concern was how to do the ceremony in the same room as the reception while also adhering to my client's dream of an entirely different look for each portion of the wedding. My client wanted a floral decor that was profuse and original. Yet there would be the space of only an hour — during which time the guests would adjourn to a separate cocktail area — to transform the room. However, given that the hostess was inviting 350 people, all the tables needed to be set well beforehand, since this in itself is a most time-consuming process.

Our solution was to create printed screens and embellish them with fresh flowers. We copied traditional details of the room for the screens for a trompe l'oeil effect, then added the flowers. Fresh flowers bursting from a two-dimensional surface creates quite a lot of tension and interest, as it juxtaposes the organic with the static image on the screen. We used these to cordon off the area for the ceremony and transform the look of the space. All the preset tables were hidden behind the screens. Then we created a traditional wedding aisle by lining it with standing brass candelabras with electric candles festooned with garlands of cream and pastel blooms. The candelabras were easy to set up and, more important, easy to remove when it came time for the reception. At the altar, the wedding canopy was a floral arch of spirea and viburnum branches.

Transforming the Room

The key element in transforming this room was the draping that covered the room's ceiling. It concealed what was to come: the ceiling was awash in flowers for the reception. We had built a grid structure across the room's ceiling from which hung hundreds of rambling roses and wisteria. By necessity we installed and decorated this first — it took nearly twenty-four hours — and then

hid it by draping it. Fastened with Velcro, the pastel green draping was quickly and easily removed as soon as the guests left the room for the cocktail area. Then we put the screens to good use by lining the corridor that led to the Grand Ballroom with them. As the guests returned for the reception, the presence of the screens lining the way seemed to announce that something quite extraordinary was waiting in store.

When guests entered the Grand Ballroom they were amazed to discover that it looked entirely different. To them, something magical had just occurred. It had been transformed into a wonderland of flowers and sparkling light. The ceiling decoration — a boldly dramatic statement — alone was breathtaking. Large magnificent centerpieces in pinks and purples and numerous pillar candles in a variety of heights graced each table. For variety and as a bit of whimsy, some centerpieces were candelabras and others were topiaries set in gilt containers. A shimmering beaded floral organza covered the tables and chairs. At every place setting, gently enveloped by the napkin, was a perfect nosegay, a gift for each guest. And as the crowning finish to a singularly romantic evening, thanks to projection, the ceiling was transformed into a night sky filled with stars.

A VISION IN
WHITE AND PINK

Ellen Caplan is a woman of extraordinary taste who knows exactly what she wants. Her vision and meticulous attention to detail are part of the success she has achieved as the operator of a highly regarded New York catering firm. When she asked me to create the decor for her daughter's wedding, I knew the result would be a statement of elegance and style. Describing her daughter as a beautifully soft woman, she wanted the decor of the wedding to reflect this. She envisioned a wedding in traditional pinks and whites, one with a soft, feminine, romantic mood. Nevertheless, she also wanted the decor to be contemporary, with simple, clean lines. Not a woman to do anything in a typical way, Mrs. Caplan put her own indelible stamp on every detail, and the result was a unique and unforgettable wedding. One of the challenges of this event was that Mrs. Caplan's vision was of a wedding based around flowering branches such as cherry or dogwood—and the wedding was being held in July, a time when that type of flower isn't available. Working together we found wonderfully creative and interesting ways to compensate, and the results were more than could have been hoped for.

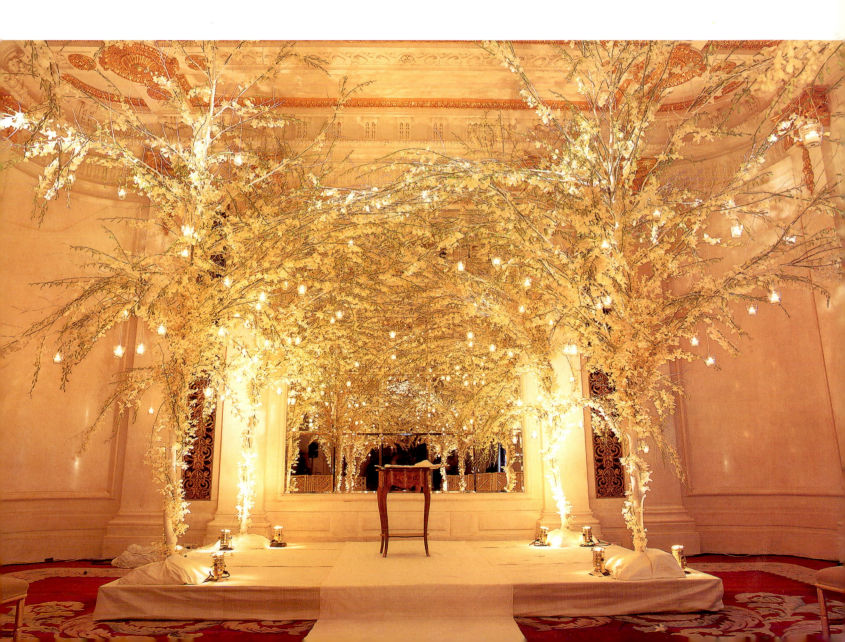

The Venue

The St. Regis Hotel was chosen as the venue for the wedding. The room where the reception was held is considered one of the most beautiful in New York, known for its ornate classical detailing. Though Mrs. Caplan's vision was all about cleanness, she loved the idea of juxtaposing a traditional room with a more contemporary event decor. While some people, such as the client in the previous example, prefer a different mood, decor, or floral design for different areas or sections of an event, Mrs. Caplan likes continuity and repetition. She wanted all the decor details to be repeated throughout the event so that the same feeling or mood would grace the entire proceedings, from the ceremony to the dancing. Both approaches have their charms and it is interesting to compare them.

The Decor

For the ceremony aisle, to approximate cherry and other spring blossoms, we used white tree branches adorned with masses of white dendrobium orchids. From the branches we hung votives, which produced a gentle, captivating glow along the aisle. The repetition of hundreds of strands of dendrobium orchids was a spectacularly romantic effect — one that might have been lost had cherry blossoms been available! For continuity, we also placed similar votive-laden branches covered with orchids around the dance floor at the reception.

The wedding's themes became clear at the escort table as a mass of peonies greeted guests. Each of the place cards on a beaded, light-rose-colored tablecloth was accompanied by a single cymbidium orchid. The orchid foreshadowed the overall look for the evening: the wedding's floral decor

was composed almost entirely of dendrobium and cymbidium orchids, the most lovely and feminine of flowers. Even the mantelpiece in the cocktail area was bedecked with masses of them. Elsewhere in the cocktail area, perfect, clear trumpet-shaped vases contained more peonies.

The Tables

Each dining table at the reception was a masterpiece. Every detail, from the centerpiece to the silverware placement, had been carefully considered so as not to succumb to convention. The palest blue silk adorned with embroidery reminiscent of dotted swiss was used for the table overlays. Crisply starched linen napkins with matching detailing were folded in threes and placed on the left of each charger. In a highly visual and unusual placement, the silverware was arranged on top of the napkin in a step pattern. On the right side of the charger sat an exquisitely decorated gift box, wrapped in hydrangea petals and topped with cymbidium orchids. At Mrs. Caplan's suggestion, white feathers, delicate enough for angel's wings, were used as trim. The boxes contained candied almonds, a traditional wedding gift—some say because they are considered to be symbols of fertility.

In their design and size, the tables' centerpieces were intended to be unique and dramatic. Made of white dendrobium orchids and accented with pink cymbidiums, each table's centerpiece was a work

of floral art designed to look like a large gift box. They were even "wrapped" with a large delicately translucent blue ribbon. Believing that most people at parties do not talk across the table to one another anyway, Mrs. Caplan went against convention by placing such oversize arrangements on the tables. For her, the more important thing was the statement she was trying to achieve with the look of them and their fit in the overall decor of the room. The lady is open to new ideas.

The silverware was set on the tables in a wonderfully original way, and also note how beautifully all the silver on the table works together. From the filigree water goblets to the chargers to the votive candle holders to the silverware, each piece is in perfect harmony with the others. The eclectic silver filigree votives have the same pattern as the chargers and the goblets. Meanwhile the simplicity and smooth lines of the pillar candleholders provide the perfect complement to the filigree. Here is yet another perfectly executed detail.

This is what can be achieved with a few colors, pale blue, rose pink, and white; a simple choice of flowers, orchids; the use of repetition; an eye for design; and a love of detail. For the hostess the evening was a huge success; she had fully enveloped her guests in her carefully designed ambience, one of magic and romance, and more important, she had given her daughter the wedding of her dreams.

A JOINT BIRTHDAY
CELEBRATION
IN PINK AND BLUE

To celebrate their joint fiftieth birthdays, my clients Eric and Harriet Rothfeld planned an extravagant birthday party for their friends and family. Mrs. Rothfeld is a woman with a wonderful confidence in her sense of style and her own instincts. And in what she loves—the colors pink and blue. The interior design of her country home in the Hamptons consists entirely of these two colors. While this may sound extreme, in truth her home is exquisite, and the originality and creativity that went into finding even the smallest decorative detail in these colors is totally outstanding. In fact, I think part of the fun for Mrs. Rothfeld is the challenge of finding items with these colors that also work perfectly in her home. Interior designer Bill Diamond worked with her to give her home its pink-and-blue French provincial look.

For their party, the Rothfelds raised a tent on their property, but they didn't want it to seem like a tent. Instead, they wanted their guests to feel as though they had been invited into the couple's home by literally continuing the decor of their home into the tent. So exacting were their specifications, they actually had me re-create design details from the house. What a magnificent idea and what a wonderful challenge!

Transforming the Room

We began by very nearly building a whole room within the tent itself. Because the couple's dining room contains latticelike architectural finishing, we framed in new walls within the tent by building wooden panels with latticework for a decorative effect. Hundreds of yards of fabric were specially printed to match a toile in the house, some of which was used to drape the ceiling. Some of the panels that made up the walls of the room contained faux windows, which we draped with curtains. Other panels had digital prints in pink and blue, including replications of vases that the couple actually owns. Exploding from these prints were masses of fresh flowers, adding considerable texture to the room overall. We also created a roofed structure to house the band and cover the dance floor. The colors of the pink and blue paint were specially mixed to match swatches from the Rothfeld's home.

Essentially the entire interior of the tent was covered. What wasn't covered with panels was draped. So when you walked into the tent you were transported into an entirely new space, like a room in the couple's home, and there was no hint of being in a tent. Even the faux windows were backlighted such that it seemed as though you were looking outside on a starry night. I don't think I fully understood at first what Mrs. Rothfeld had in mind, how far she intended to go to achieve her vision of this extension of her home. We engaged in quite a bit of trial and error, yet she was unequivocal in what she wanted and was involved every step of the way.

The Entrance

Because we wanted the event to be perfect, we created an entrance to the tent that again was made to look as though it were the foyer of a home. The party celebrated the couple's joint one hundred years of life, but it also celebrated their union — they've known each other since junior high school. So we placed a sepia-toned enlargement of the couple's wedding photo in the entranceway together with a table holding a number of other personal photos from different stages of their lives. Scented candles and four large, gorgeous spiraling topiaries also greeted the guests. The entire effect of the foyer was to embrace the partygoers warmly and bring them into the family fold.

Then you walked into the tent. We balanced the blue walls by painting the wooden floor laid down for the event in pink. The dance floor was a stroke of creative genius. It is a replica of a custom carpet produced for the main hallway of the house with the couple's initials in the center. Michael Speir digitally printed the image of the carpet on vinyl for the dance floor.

The Tables

This same specially printed fabric used throughout the room for draping was used for the table overlays, some in pink and some in blue. We also re-created a buffalo plaid found in the couple's home for the table underlays and seat covers. The tables alternated all blue overlays, underlays, and seat covers with all pink ones. The place settings for the tables were delicious. Fond of a classical look, Mrs. Rothfeld wanted the tables to look traditional. Beautiful white porcelain china with a blue floral motif sat on cobalt blue chargers next to cut crystal stemware. The pedestals and finials in the shape of urns on the tables were painted with specially created paint. A great globe of hydrangeas and roses was the perfect combination of blooms to achieve all pink and blue floral arrangements. Each place setting was graced with either a pink or a blue hydrangea. In some ways, the tables gave the impression that this was a garden party.

The Details

No detail was left unattended to. The table numbers, hand painted and decorated with blooms, fit the overall scheme beautifully. Even the invitations were tied with a perfect blue ribbon flown in from London. In case the day threatened rain, the hostess thoughtfully provided guests with — what else — pink umbrellas sitting at the ready in pink-and-blue baskets.

Not one of the 250 people who came away from this event left untouched. Everyone had a marvelous time, and I understand that this party is still being talked about. This event was a resounding success for many of the reasons I've tried to share with you in this book. As I've said, this is a couple with a wonderfully clear vision. Mrs. Rothfeld is unapologetic about what makes her happy. And so she kept her sights on what she wanted throughout the planning process and right down to the tiniest of details. More than that, she based her decisions on what made her comfortable, which in turn meant that her guests would be comfortable. It was pure generosity on the part of this couple to want to share the most intimate details of their home with the people attending their celebration and to go to such lengths to do so.

Above all else, both Mr. and Mrs. Rothfeld approached this event with a childlike abandon and exuberant joy. They couldn't help but infect every detail of the party with this energy and, in turn, communicate this to their guests. Installing the decor of this party was a two-week process, preceded by months of planning. The Rothfelds were genuinely excited to be part of the transformation. It was wonderful to work with clients that were so open to experimentation and doing things a bit differently. And clearly their excitement was communicated to their guests. Everyone who experienced it felt that this was no ordinary celebration but one of the most incredible parties they had ever attended.

Many thanks to everyone at Preston Bailey Design, including (*seated from left to right*): Shereese Charles, Receptionist; Silomar Balbino, Transportation; Regina Evans, Director of Administration. *Standing from left to right:* Luiz Fernando Silva, Director of Operations; Marcos Vinagre, Designer; Darci Vazquez, Assistant Operations Manager; Kurt Gibson, Florist; Oscar Simeon Jr., Senior Florist; Nadine Jervis, Office Manager; Sanaw Ledrod, Designer.

$\mathscr{A}$CKNOWLEDGMENTS

First, I want to thank Michael Speir for all his love and his gift of incredible attention to detail. Also, my thanks go to my longtime friend Bill Ash for his wonderful advice and support.

My gratitude goes to Regina Evans, my right-hand assistant, whose dedication and extraordinary organizational skills have contributed so much to Preston Bailey Design.

In addition, I would like to thank Sylvia Weinstock, my friend and mentor; my friend Marcy Blum for her love; and my friends the Keidens for all their encouragement. I also thank my friends the Sterns.

Many thanks to my friends event planners Elizabeth K. Allen, Harriette Rose Katz, and Judith Schwartz.

Finally, my appreciation goes to those who helped make this book a reality, including photographers Alex Kirkbride and Roger Dong, designer Julia Sedykh, production manager Melissa Langen, Carol Judy Leslie and senior editor Dorothy Williams of Bulfinch, and Bulfinch publisher Jill Cohen.

I would also like to acknowledge the contributions of the following: Marc Muster, Designer; Jerry Sibal, Design Fusion; Aharon Elperin, Beta Ironworks, Corporation; Michael Speir, Graphic Design—Computer Imagery Consultant; Thom Lussier, Cafiero Lussier Caterers; Digital Dirigible, Digital Printing; Casper Hargreaves Studio, Lanterns; Bentley Meeker Lighting & Staging, Inc.; Jerry Schwartz, House of Schwartz; Dara Wishingrad, Art Director; Tangram International Exhibitions, Inc.; Karen Speir, Product Development; Larry Speir, Builder; Rathe Productions, Inc.; Orlando Palacios, Builder; Frost Lighting.

First edition

Photographs by Roger Dong, with
additional photography by Alex Kirkbride.

Library of Congress Control Number
2002102347

Bulfinch Press is a division of AOL Time
Warner Book Group.

Printed in Singapore